A CURIOUS GUIDE TO LONDON

www.transworldbooks.co.uk

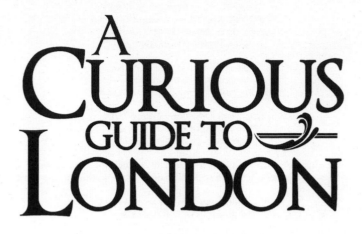

A CURIOUS GUIDE TO LONDON

TALES OF A CITY

SIMON LEYLAND

BANTAM PRESS

LONDON • TORONTO • SYDNEY • AUCKLAND • JOHANNESBURG

TRANSWORLD PUBLISHERS
61–63 Uxbridge Road, London W5 5SA
A Random House Group Company
www.transworldbooks.co.uk

First published in Great Britain
in 2014 by Bantam Press
an imprint of Transworld Publishers

Copyright © Simon Leyland 2014
Maps copyright © Patrick Mulrey
Illustrations by Micaela Alcaino

Simon Leyland has asserted his right under the Copyright,
Designs and Patents Act 1988 to be identified as the author of this work.

A CIP catalogue record for this book
is available from the British Library.

ISBN 9780593073230

Addresses for Random House Group Ltd companies outside the UK
can be found at: www.randomhouse.co.uk
The Random House Group Ltd Reg. No. 954009

The Random House Group Limited supports the Forest Stewardship
Council® (FSC®), the leading international forest-certification organisation.
Our books carrying the FSC label are printed on FSC®-certified paper. FSC
is the only forest-certification scheme supported by the leading environmental
organisations, including Greenpeace. Our paper procurement policy can be
found at www.randomhouse.co.uk/environment

Typeset in 9.5/13 pt Berling Roman by Falcon Oast Graphic Art Ltd
Printed and bound in Great Britain by
Clays Ltd, Bungay, Suffolk

2 4 6 8 10 9 7 5 3

You are now
In London, that great sea, whose ebb and flow
At once is deaf and loud, and on the shore
Vomits its wrecks, and still howls on for more.
Yet in its depth what treasures!

Letter to Maria Gisborne, 1820
Percy Bysshe Shelley

CONTENTS

Marylebone

Mayfair

Piccadilly

St James's

St Paul's

The City and the East End

Tower Hill

Greenwich

Sources and Further Reading

Acknowledgements

INTRODUCTION

This collection of tales can be blamed on a London Underground strike, a rainy evening and a pub in Moorgate.

A few years ago, when I was still pretending to enjoy life in the Square Mile, I was walking along London Wall on the way to Moorgate Underground station when the heavens opened. Quickly dashing through the puddles, I discovered the entrance closed due to a previously unannounced strike. As is the way when it rains in London, there are never any taxis to be found; and when there is a tube strike, it is almost impossible to get on a bus. So I did what any responsible adult would do: I decided to get out of the rain and go to a pub for a pint or two while I reviewed my options.

The pub was strangely quiet considering the time of day and the events unfurling outside. I ordered a pint and sat down at the bar looking at the rain through the window. No sooner had I taken my first sip than a slightly dishevelled elderly man wearing an Evening Standard waterproof jacket sat down beside me and started talking to me as if I were a long-lost friend.

I initially thought the poor old sod was one of life's unfortunates, but how wrong can you be. His name was Alf, he had been selling newspapers on the corner of London Wall and Moorgate for over twenty years, and he started to regale me with stories of a London that I never knew. The man was a born storyteller, and in return for several light and bitters, he kept me amused until closing time, when I bade him farewell and left for home.

I had assumed that his anecdotes were all tall tales and completely dismissed them from my thoughts until a chance meeting at a dinner party, when I was introduced to a rather severe-looking fellow who claimed to be a local historian. Remembering my encounter with Alf, I asked him about a couple of the stories he had told me. They were in fact all totally true.

The following Monday, I made my way back along London Wall to reacquaint myself with my new friend, but he was nowhere to be seen. I subsequently discovered that the day I met him had been his last day at work.

With my interest piqued, I started to research the subject and was amazed at how many little-known stories and curious tales London had to offer – hardly surprising considering the city has been around for over two thousand years, has burned down several times, been rebuilt, been bombed in two world wars and been rebuilt again.

There are many books about London, and if you are looking for a scholarly treatise on the history of this great city I fear you must look elsewhere. Likewise, if you were expecting an earnest discussion on the social fabric of London you will be sorely disappointed.

This book is unashamedly light-hearted and has been written for people like myself who take delight in the strange and absurd – such as where Rimbaud hit Verlaine with a fish; why you can't tell the time in Bermondsey; the location of Farting Lane; and where a man was killed by a falling penis.

What follows are the results of my beer-fuelled endeavours. I hope it delights, astonishes and fascinates in equal measure, and that it inspires you to look at the city in a new light.

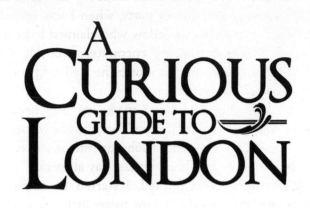

KENSINGTON
and CHELSEA

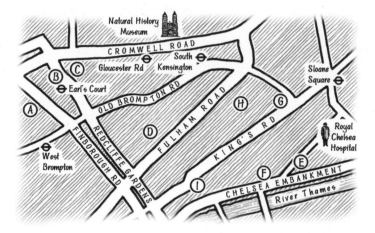

The First London Eye

☞ *Earls Court Exhibition Centre, Warwick Road*
MAP: A

The first giant Ferris wheel in London was erected for the Empire of India Exhibition at Earls Court in 1894.

Built by two young Australian engineers named Adam Gaddelin and Gareth Watson, the Great Wheel, as it was known, was modelled on the original Ferris wheel that had appeared in Chicago the year before. It was 300 feet high (compared with 442 feet for the London Eye today) and was capable of carrying twelve hundred passengers in its forty carriages. The wheel caused enormous excitement and it remained in use for several years. On the evening of 6 May 1906, however, it got stuck and seventy-four people in the upper carriages who could not climb down had to stay there all night. Tea and sandwiches were hoisted up and the unlucky passengers were finally brought down by the fire brigade the following morning. There followed a splendid rumour that the Victorian equivalent of the Mile High Club had gained its first members. As a result, an employee with a pair of binoculars was tasked with spying on the carriages to make sure no impropriety took place.

The wheel stayed in service until later that year, by which time it had carried over 2.5 million passengers.

Bumper Harris and Escalator Etiquette

☞ *Earl's Court Underground Station, Earls Court Road*
MAP: B

The inaugural London Underground line opened in January 1863 between Paddington and Farringdon, and was the first of its kind in the world.

In 1910 the tube introduced its first escalator at Earl's Court station. Passengers initially were very wary of it, so in order to prove the safety of this new contraption the Underground operators came up with the novel idea of employing someone to ride the escalator all day. So began the career of Bumper Harris, a man with a wooden leg – thereby demonstrating that if it was safe for a man with a disability, then it was safe for all – who continued to go up and down for several years until the public eventually took to these new moving staircases.

In many countries, escalator etiquette demands that travellers stand on the left and walk on the right, but on the London Underground it has always been the other way round. A

recently restored silent film from the 1920s may explain why. *Underground*, the first film to feature extensive footage of the tube, shows that due to the design of early escalators it was necessary to step off with the right foot. Unlike modern comb escalators, where the end of the stairway is straight, older shunt escalators ended in a diagonal so the stairway finished sooner for the right foot than for the left. Passengers who chose not to walk up or down the escalators were therefore asked to stand on the right so that anyone wishing to overtake them at the end would be able to take advantage of the extra section of moving stairway.

And as a result, the convention of standing on the right has been fiercely enforced by the travelling public ever since – as many an unsuspecting tourist who has stood on the left during rush hour can testify.

Corpse Candles

☞ *Hogarth Road*
MAP: C

The autumn of 1835 saw the introduction of a new type of candle called the 'composition candle'. It burned cleanly, but at the same cost as the inferior tallow candle, which was made from animal fat and tended to splutter when burning.

These new candles were created by Joseph Gay-Lussac and Michel Chevreul, two French scientists, who separated tallow into two parts: one liquid, and one solid which they called 'stearine'. The stearine had a higher melting point than crude tallow and a secret ingredient was added to prevent the candles becoming brittle. The Frenchmen sold their 'secret' recipe to Warner & Sons of Hogarth Road, who became very prosperous through the manufacture of these candles.

One night, however, a London chemist, a Mr Everitt, was extinguishing his candle when he noticed an 'abominable stinking smell like garlic, the characteristic smell given off by arsenical vapours'.

The Westminster Medical Society conducted an investigation and concluded that the 'secret' ingredient was in fact arsenic – odourless while the candle burned, the smell only being released when it was snuffed out. The society then put forward the following scenario: 'What if London's Theatre Royal, Drury Lane were lighted with stearine candles [each chandelier held 152 tapers] ... 608 grains of arsenious acid would be vaporised and floating in the air during the performance. Is anyone prepared to assert that [no one] would receive the slightest injury?' Composition candles were banned the following year.

Somewhat bizarrely, although it had long been well known as a poison, doctors for centuries had prescribed arsenic for their patients, and in 1809 Fowler's Solution, a mixture of potassium arsenite and lavender commonly taken as a tonic, was accepted into the London Pharmacopoeia and was praised by the *Edinburgh Medical and Surgical Journal* as 'almost as certain a medicine as we possess throughout the whole range of our materia medica'. It also appears that it was popular amongst certain men who took it in the hope of increasing 'energy, endurance and virility' in the bedroom.

Incredibly, lessons had not been learned. The arsenic problem returned again in 1859, only this time in the form of a colouring used for home furnishings and fabric – Scheele's Green. People dropped like flies after having their drawing rooms re-papered in 'the rage for green', which *Punch* came to call 'the hue of death, the tint of the grave'. There were reports of children wasting away in bright green rooms, of ladies in green dresses swooning, and newspaper printers being overcome by arsenic vapours. Many scholars believe that Napoleon's death in St Helena in 1821 was due to the green wallpaper in his bedroom.

The Tichborne Claimant

☞ *14 Harley Gardens*

MAP: D

This is where Arthur Orton, also known as Sir Roger Tichborne, lived during his trial as the Tichborne Claimant – a story which has all the elements of a Victorian melodrama.

In 1854, whilst on a sea voyage, a wealthy young aristocrat named Roger Charles Doughty Tichborne disappeared and was presumed dead. His mother, refusing to believe he had actually died, placed advertisements in newspapers around the world seeking information on his whereabouts. In the spring of 1866 she received a letter from an Australian man in Wagga Wagga who claimed to be her son. Thus began one of the greatest mysteries of the time.

There were significant differences between the Australian claimant and Roger Tichborne. Tichborne was very slight of figure and spoke fluent French when he disappeared. The man from Wagga Wagga weighed over twenty stone, spoke no French and had a very pronounced Australian accent. However, there was a facial resemblance between the two.

Lady Tichborne embraced the Australian man as her long-lost son, making him the full heir to her estate. But upon her death, the family took legal action to prevent him from accessing the inheritance. What followed was one of the most sensational trials of the Victorian age. At a time when very few people owned any form of personal documentation, the case hinged on his proving his identity in a court of law.

Investigators were sent to Australia and alleged that the claimant was in fact a butcher's son from Wapping called Arthur Orton, who had moved to Australia. Under cross-examination, he proved unable to remember the simplest facts about the past of Roger Tichborne. The court ruled in the family's favour and in 1874 the Tichborne Claimant was convicted on two counts of perjury and sentenced to fourteen years' hard labour.

He served ten years in prison before being released in 1884. For the next couple of years he travelled around the music halls trying to make a living from his celebrity status, but eventually interest in the case waned and Orton lived out the rest of his life in near poverty, still claiming to be Sir Roger right up until his death in 1898.

It seems almost certain that the Australian man was a fraud, but when he died the family allowed the name 'Sir Roger Charles Doughty Tichborne' to be inscribed on his tombstone.

———— • ————

The Physic Garden and *The Day of the Triffids*

☞ *66 Royal Hospital Road*
MAP: E

During the Second World War, whilst working as a censor at the Ministry of Information, the writer John Wyndham used to come to the Chelsea Physic Garden for his lunch breaks.

One particular lunchtime he was said to have seen a strange-looking shrub which later formed the idea of the 'triffid' in his bestselling book *The Day of the Triffids*, published in 1951.

Established as a nursery for trainee apothecaries in 1673, the Chelsea Physic Garden is the second oldest botanical garden in Britain, after the University of Oxford Botanic Garden, which was founded in 1621.

In 1732 cotton seeds from the garden were sent to James Oglethorpe, founder of the state of Georgia, who used them to establish the American cotton industry.

Giant's Teeth and Job's Tears

☞ *18 Cheyne Walk*
MAP: F

London's first public museum opened in a coffee house on this site, near Chelsea Old Church, in 1695.

It was originally a barber's shop whose proprietor, James Salter – or Don Saltero, as he later became known – had once been employed as travelling valet to Sir Hans Sloane, whose collection formed the basis of the British Museum. Sloane began to donate unwanted objects to Salter, who took them to his shop, displayed them in cabinets around the walls and invited the public to come in.

As word about the collection spread, the barber's shop evolved into Don Saltero's Coffee House and Curiosity Museum. He promoted it as a place of marvels and wonder, as an advertisement placed in *Mist's Weekly Journal* in 1728 shows:

> Monsters of all sorts here are seen,
> Strange things in Nature as they grew so,
> Some relics of the Sheba Queen,
> And fragments of the famed Bob Crusoe.
> Knick-knacks, too, dangle round the wall,
> Some in glass-cases, some on shelf,
> But what's the rarest sight of all?
> **YOUR HUMBLE SERVANT SHOWS HIMSELF.**

Among the exhibits were: a giant's tooth; a curious piece of metal found in the ruins of Troy; the Pope's infallible candle; manna from Canaan; a necklace made of Job's tears; a leprechaun's foreskin; and a sandal that belonged to Pontius Pilate's wife.

There was no charge to see the museum, but visitors were expected to buy a cup of coffee or a catalogue for twopence. Poor old Salter was evidently not a good businessman. After a few years he declared bankruptcy and the museum closed. The entire contents were auctioned off in 1799.

Mr Crapper's Bottom Slapper

☞ *120 King's Road*
MAP: G

Thomas Crapper, sanitary pioneer and inventor – though not, contrary to popular belief, the actual inventor of the flushing toilet (see page 176) – was born in Yorkshire in 1836, the son of a sailor. He apparently walked all the way to London to begin an apprenticeship with a plumber and when he had completed his training he set up on his own in 1861 on Robert Street, Chelsea.

Success quickly followed and five years later he took a lease on some larger premises, the Marlboro' Works in nearby Marlborough Road, which he used as his workshop; then in 1907 he opened his first shop here on the King's Road.

Crapper relentlessly promoted sanitary fittings to a some-what sceptical world and championed the 'water-waste-preventing cistern syphon' in particular. He also invented the idea of the bathroom showroom when he fitted out the Marlboro' Works with large plate-glass windows to show the passing public his wares. But as with so many things, this was too much for Victorian sensibilities; the sight of so many toilet bowls on show caused several ladies to faint.

Crapper registered a number of patents, one of which was for the 'disconnecting trap' which became an essential underground drain fitting. But perhaps the most interesting was his spring-loaded toilet seat, which was designed to flush automatically once the user stood up. Unfortunately, due to a problem with the rubber buffers on the underside of the seat, the seat would remain down, attached to the toilet bowl, for a few seconds as the user got to his feet. Then the powerful springs would release the seat, which would immediately slap the unfortunate incumbent on the bare bottom.

The device became popularly known as the 'Bottom Slapper'

and, unsurprisingly, seems not to have been a commercial success.

Sadly, the word 'crap' is not derived from Thomas Crapper's name, as is so often supposed. Its origins are more likely to be a Middle English combination of the Dutch word *krappen*, meaning to pluck off, cut off or separate, and the Old French *crappe*, meaning waste or rejected matter. It was first used in relation to human waste in 1846, according to the *Oxford English Dictionary*, in the term 'crapping ken', meaning a privy.

Mr Crapper seems to have approached his business with a sense of humour. All his porcelain urinals carried the tiny logo of a bee. For the bee in Latin is *apis* – a piss!

———— • ————

The Batman of Chelsea

☞ *Sydney Street*
MAP: H

On the afternoon of 20 June 1874, a hot-air balloon was seen hovering over Chelsea with what appeared to be a gigantic bat dangling beneath it. Perched inside was the wonderfully bonkers Vincent de Groof, otherwise known as 'the Flying Man'. He was convinced that he could fly using a machine fitted with large wings and a tiller, an invention that had been pioneered by the Frenchman Jean Pierre François Blanchard a century earlier. These machines were known as 'ornithopters' and de Groof's version consisted of an enclosed cabin in which he would pedal away furiously while a complicated array of gears powered the flapping wings.

The balloon and de Groof had taken off from Cremorne Gardens, now the site of Lots Road Power Station. At that time, Cremorne Gardens was known as a place of entertainment and had previously featured balloonists and parachutists.

The plan was that, at some point in the flight, de Groof would cut the rope and pedal his machine back to earth. After hovering over the Thames for some time, the balloon pilot descended to around three hundred feet in preparation for de Groof's solo flight, but the bat machine swung unnervingly close to the tower of St Luke's Church, just north of the King's Road.

Presumably concerned that he would hit the tower, de Groof then cut the rope. His airborne pedalo immediately toppled over and the unfortunate fellow tumbled to the ground, landing in Sydney Street where he died instantly.

The balloon, released of its burden, shot upwards to such a height that the pilot lost consciousness. It eventually landed on a railway line just outside Chingford, narrowly missing a train.

———————— • ————————

London's First 'Artificial Ice' Rink

☞ *Milman's Street*
MAP: I

The world's first artificially frozen ice rink opened in 1876 in a tent off the King's Road in Chelsea.

Three decades earlier, in 1844, there had been a short-lived attempt at indoor skating when a small rink was created at the Baker Street Bazaar near Portman Square. The 'ice' had been a mixture of hog's lard and chemical salts, but its popularity had quickly waned because of the smell of cheese wafting from the surface on warm days.

The question of how to bring indoor skating to the Victorians was eventually answered by John Gamgee, who some years earlier had developed and patented a method of freezing meat so that it could be imported from Australia and New Zealand. Now he applied his experience to creating artificial ice. Over a base of concrete covered with earth, cow's hair and wooden planks he laid a series of copper pipes. These were covered with water, which was frozen by a solution of glycerine, nitrogen peroxide, ether and water pumped through the pipes.

Gamgee decorated the walls of his Glaciarium, as it was known, with Alpine views and above the ice he built a gallery that could be used by an orchestra or by spectators. He operated the rink as a kind of members' club for wealthy people; most of them were already experienced open-air skaters as a result of spending their winters in the Alps.

Initially the venture proved very popular and Gamgee soon opened several more rinks around the country. However, problems with the freezing technique caused a mist to rise from the surface, which proved offputting for skaters, and by the end of the decade all the Glaciaria had closed.

PADDINGTON
AND HYDE PARK

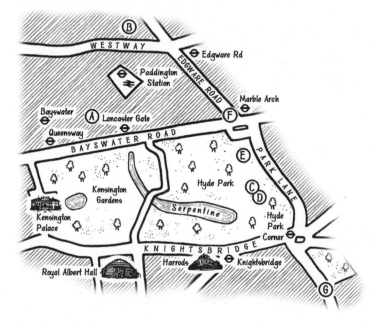

The False Houses of Paddington

☞ *23–24 Leinster Terrace*
MAP: *A*

When work began on the London Underground, the first line was set to run from Paddington to Farringdon. For the excavations to take place, several houses would have to be purchased then demolished. Some property agents, seeing a chance to make a killing, raised the values of their buildings, most notably at 23 and 24 Leinster Terrace.

The Railway Commissioners had no choice but to buy the buildings at the inflated prices, however, as this was a point on the Underground line where a ventilation shaft was needed. The first Underground trains were steam-driven and safety demanded that every so often a place should be provided where they could vent off their steam and smoke well away from a station.

In view of the area's upmarket status, when the Underground construction work was finished it was decided to restore the uniformity of the street with its five-storey townhouses by rebuilding the façades of numbers 23 and 24. These beautiful, Georgian-style walls, complete with doors and windows, therefore conceal nothing but a large cavity and the grids covering the ventilation shaft. A famous hoax in the 1930s saw a cheeky fraudster make a small fortune by selling ten-guinea tickets for a charity ball here. It was only when the excited guests, in full evening dress, knocked on the fake door that they realized they had been duped.

Shillibeer's Parisian Omnibus

☞ *Paddington Green*
MAP: B

In July 1829 George Shillibeer revolutionized London's transport by starting the first regular public bus service. He was inspired by the French, who already had bus services in Paris, and he was careful to stress the French name *omnibus* in his advertising. Crowds gathered in Paddington Green to cheer the first omnibus, 'running upon the Parisian mode', as it set out. Three horses pulled the twenty-two passengers who, for a fare of one shilling and sixpence (the equivalent of £3.59 today), were taken to Bank via The Angel, Islington.

Attended by a conductor – 'a person of great respectability' – Shillibeer's two omnibuses left Paddington and the City respectively at three-hourly intervals. The fares were less than those for the short-stage coaches, no advance booking was required, and passengers were picked up anywhere en route.

This new bus service proved so popular that within a year there were six rival companies. Within three years, ninety buses were running on the Paddington–Bank route, and there was another service between Hammersmith and Somerset House.

Most omnibuses were licensed to carry fifteen passengers inside, while four others sat on the roof by the driver. The buses had wood shavings on the floor and people sat on benches along each side. On an outside step stood the conductor who collected the fares and kept the bus as full as possible.

To stop the bus, you banged on the roof or prodded the conductor. This simple method was soon replaced by a bell, and one company used a device of two leather straps attached to the driver's arms. Passengers pulled on either the left or right 'rein' to indicate on which side of the road they wanted to be put down.

By 1835 there were six hundred buses operating in the capital. By this stage Shillibeer was elderly, and the stress of running the company and dealing with his increasingly competitive rivals was making him ill. So the man who had pioneered the 'commute' bowed out. He was not finished, however. He turned his buses into hearses and 'Shillibeer's Original Omnibuses' became 'Shillibeer's Funeral Coaches'.

———— • ————

The Petticoat Duel

☞ *Hyde Park*
MAP: C

In 1792 Lady Almeria Braddock took umbrage over a remark about her age made by a Mrs Elphinstone, so she challenged the younger lady to a duel in Hyde Park.

Over two hundred people were present to watch Lady Braddock's hat blown off by a pistol shot and Mrs Elphinstone wounded in the arm during the subsequent sword fight.

Hostilities ceased at this point, with Mrs Elphinstone agreeing to apologize. The ladies curtsied to each other, then left for tea.

Cycling Chaperones, Hygienic Saddles and Toulouse-Lautrec

☞ *Hyde Park*
MAP: D

The Victorians loved new fads and inventions, and it was in Hyde Park in the summer of 1896 that the cycling craze really took off. Not everybody admired bicycling, however. There were many who considered the machines to be the 'invention of the devil', as Swithin Forsyte in John Galsworthy's *The Forsyte Saga* called them after a 'penny farthing had startled his greys at Brighton in 1884'.

When Hyde Park first opened its gates to cyclists in October 1890, they were allowed to ride in the park only up to midday. The last thing people expected was that just six years later there would be in excess of three thousand cyclists – mainly women, wearing long, heavy skirts, bonnets and gloves – taking part in a parade around the park.

The rate at which women took up cycling seemed to surprise everybody and many articles appeared in the newspapers and periodicals foretelling the dangers. Critics warned that ladies risked both their health and their mental stability by cycling, endangering their hair, complexions, femininity, families, morals and, worst of all, their reputations. One commentator argued that 'cycling heats the blood . . . destroys feminine symmetry and poise' and is 'a disturber of internal organs'.

In order to keep indecency at bay, the Chaperone Cyclists' Association was formed and supplied female escorts for solo women cyclists for three shillings an hour. Also available, and designed to avoid blushes, was the Pattison Hygienic Cycle Saddle, which had a modest dip in the area where a lady's crotch would usually meet the seat. It also claimed to remove the major drawback in cycling, namely 'perineal pressure'.

Watching the proceedings that summer was the brothel-loving artist Henri de Toulouse-Lautrec. He was a cycling fan, and had been asked by a company called Simpson to design a poster for their bike, which used a new type of chain. The famous poster he produced in 1896 was one of his last; he died five years later, just as the Victorian cycling craze was coming to an end.

———— • ————

Lenin and his Irish Accent

☞ *Speakers' Corner*
MAP: E

A small piece of land at the north-east corner of Hyde Park has come to symbolize freedom of speech and the right of assembly. Known as Speakers' Corner, it is famous throughout the world and, since the great Victorian reformers first held their rallies here, countless men and women from all walks of life have stood at this spot to proclaim their views and win support for their causes.

Amongst them, in 1902, was the young Russian revolutionary Vladimir Lenin, who was living in London with his wife. Anxious to learn English in order to communicate his beliefs, he placed an advertisement in *The Times* to the effect that 'if you help teach me English, I'll help teach you Russian'. An English tutor, originally from Rathmines in Dublin, took him up on his offer.

The consequence was that the father of the Soviet Union learned to speak English with an Irish accent – as confirmed in an article written by *War of the Worlds* author H. G. Wells, who met Lenin in Moscow in 1920 and noticed his Irish brogue.

So, rather amusingly, when Paddy Vladimir O'Lenin was haranguing the crowds at Speakers' Corner about the evils of capitalism, he was doing so in an Irish accent.

The Tyburn Tree

☞ *Bayswater Road, London*
MAP: F

They called it 'the deadly nevergreen', the tree that bore fruit all year long.

Every Monday for the last two hundred years or so of its existence, condemned men and women travelled from Newgate Prison to Tyburn, place of public execution. Set at the junction of what is now Edgware Road, Park Lane and Oxford Street, the gallows overlooked Hyde Park. Estimates of the number of people put to death here vary between forty thousand and sixty thousand.

Among the notable people who died at Tyburn were, in 1534, Elizabeth Barton, the prophesying nun; in 1541 Francis Dereham, Queen Catherine Howard's lover; and in 1724 Jack Shepherd, better known as 'Gentleman Jack', the notorious thief and escape artist.

The first execution here took place in 1196, when William Fitz Osbern was found guilty of leading the poor in an uprising; the last was of the highwayman John Austin in 1783. The first hangings were carried out from tree branches on the bank of the Tyburn River, but in 1220 a pair of gallows were built on the site. The Triple Tree (the name given to the most famous set of gallows, which allowed simultaneous hangings to take place, was built in 1571 and removed in 1759 because it was obstructing the highway. A mobile gallows was then used until hangings were moved to Newgate Prison.

There is a theory that the phrase 'on the wagon', meaning abstaining from alcohol, stems from a tradition that was already in place by the time Tyburn became a place of execution. At the bequest of Queen Matilda (wife of Henry I), a cup of charity was given to the condemned as they travelled on their last journey towards death. The wagon would stop at a tavern where each condemned person would receive a pint of ale and, after that final drink, prisoners were put back 'on the wagon', never to drink again.

The Last Crossroads Burial in England

☞ *Grosvenor Place*

MAP: G

From the introduction of Christianity to Saxon Britain in the sixth century, right up to the nineteenth century, committing suicide was regarded as a crime equalling murder and, accordingly, people who'd committed suicide could not be interred in consecrated ground. Instead, alongside other criminals, they were buried at crossroads, as the cross formed by the intersection of the roads at least brought some suggestion of religion to the site.

The last person who committed suicide to be buried in this way in Britain was a twenty-two-year-old law student named Abel Griffiths, who was interred at the crossing of Grosvenor Place and Lower Grosvenor Place in June 1823. By this time opposition to the practice was growing as understanding of mental illness and depression increased, so the crowd of spectators who turned out that day were there to protest rather than just to watch. They succeeded in holding up the carriage of George IV as they made their views known, and by this time the government was also reviewing the matter.

Crossroads burial was officially abolished later that year by the Burial of Suicides Act. For some time to come, however, the law stipulated that the bodies of those who commited suicide could be interred in consecrated ground only between the hours of 9 p.m. and midnight and strictly without the usual ceremonies accorded to the dead.

MARYLEBONE

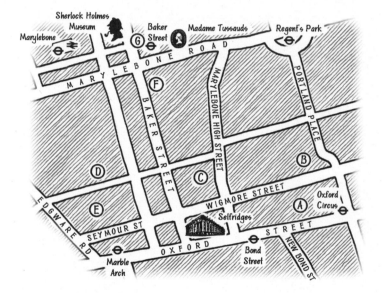

Sherlock Holmes Museum · Baker Street · Madame Tussauds · Regent's Park · Marylebone · MARYLEBONE ROAD · BAKER STREET · MARYLEBONE HIGH STREET · PORTLAND PLACE · WIGMORE STREET · Oxford Circus · Selfridges · EDGWARE RD · SEYMOUR ST · OXFORD STREET · NEW BOND ST · Marble Arch · Bond Street

The House Lost in a Game of Cards and the Nutty Duke of Portland

☞ *Harcourt House, Cavendish Square*
MAP: *A*

Harcourt House, on the western side of Cavendish Square, was a famous London mansion built for Robert Benson, Baron Bingley, on land acquired from Edward Harley, Earl of Oxford. Construction of the house began in 1721. Unusually for a central London residence at that time, the grounds included a magnificent courtyard facing the square, a large garden and vast stables.

Later the house passed into the hands of the Harcourt family, who owned it until 1825 when, incredibly, this impressive mansion was gambled away during a game of cards between the third Earl Harcourt and the third Duke of Portland.

About twenty years later, the splendidly eccentric fifth Duke of Portland, William Cavendish-Scott-Bentinck, lived here after inheriting the house. One of his 'improvements' was to enclose the garden with a gigantic screen of ground glass and cast iron, eighty feet high and extending for two hundred feet on each side, in order to prevent his neighbours from looking into his grounds.

The duke was an exceptionally shy and reclusive man, who tried to avoid people at all costs – to the extent that even when he walked from his carriage into the house, the servants would be sent elsewhere so that they couldn't look at him. Inside the house was a complicated series of bells that he could pull when he was approaching a room to warn any servant of his imminent arrival and he instructed his staff by leaving notes dotted around the house. He is perhaps most famous for the underground tunnel he constructed between his home at Welbeck Abbey and Worksop, so that he could complete most of the journey to and from London unobserved. This odd way of living meant that, unsurprisingly, he never married.

In the late nineteenth century the leasehold of Harcourt House was purchased by the Earl of Breadalbane, and on its expiration Sir William Harcourt, great-grand-nephew of the man who had lost it at cards, acquired it. It stood empty for some years, however, and was demolished in 1906.

The site of the beautiful garden, complete with screen and stables, was eventually purchased by the Post Office authorities in 1938, but was destroyed in the Blitz in 1940 by a bomb. It is now a luxury office block.

——————— • ———————

The Dancing Highwayman

☞ *Chandos Street*
MAP: *B*

It was at a tavern in Chandos Street that the career of Claude Du Vall, the famous 'gentleman highwaymen', finally came to an end. By reputation, Du Vall was gallant and courteous, one of the most dashing of all English highwayman. His contemporaries called him a 'true gentleman of the road' and 'an eternal feather in the cap of highway gentility'.

He was the son of a French miller and was born in Normandy in 1643. He became footman to an English nobleman and at the Restoration of the monarchy came to England with his master; it was probably in this service that he learned his gentle manners. By 1666, however, he had become known to the authorities as a highwayman who frequented the northern fringes of London, and the area between Highgate and Holloway in particular. Although he robbed them mercilessly, he was never violent towards his victims, and ladies of all classes loved him for his gallantry and fashionable dress.

In the best-known story about his exploits, Du Vall held up

a nobleman and his wife in their coach. Determined not to show her fear, the lady took out a flageolet (a small flute) and started to play. To her surprise, Du Vall took one out as well and joined in. He complimented the nobleman on his wife's musical ability and said he could imagine she might dance just as well. Taking her hand, he helped her down from the coach and they danced, after which he escorted her back to her seat. He then pointed out that her husband had neglected to pay for the entertainment, and promptly took four hundred guineas from him.

Du Vall was eventually captured at the Hole-in-the-Wall Tavern in Chandos Street where he was 'entertaining a lady upstairs'. He was immediately sent to Newgate Prison to await trial.

There were numerous attempts to intercede on his behalf, particularly from the ladies of the court. Even King Charles tried to intervene, but the law prevailed. Du Vall was hanged at Tyburn on 21 January 1670, aged twenty-seven. His execution drew a large and sympathetic crowd, which included several 'ladies of quality' wearing masks.

His body lay in state at the Tangier Tavern in St Giles and he was given a lavish funeral at St Paul's Church in Covent Garden, where he is buried beneath the central aisle. Part of his epitaph reads: 'Here lies Du Vall. Reader, if male thou art, look to thy purse; if female, to thy heart.'

The Pig-faced Lady of Manchester Square

☞ *Manchester Square*
MAP: C

In September 1814 Londoners were electrified by rumours of a young woman with a human body and the head of a pig who was supposedly living somewhere in Manchester Square.

According to the story, the lady was from Dublin, but after inheriting a very substantial sum had come to London in search of a husband with whom to share it. Unfortunately, her plans for marital bliss had gone awry due to her unconventional appearance and her inability to speak. She was said to communicate in grunts and would eat her meals only from a silver trough.

Within a few months, and fuelled by the popular press, the rumours had been elevated to the status of fact. A number of young men placed advertisements in the papers expressing their desire to meet London's most eligible lady and their suitability for the role of husband.

On 16 February 1815, following a letter to *The Times* from a young man asking them to publish an offer of marriage to the lady in question, the paper carried a wonderfully acerbic editorial:

> There is at present a report, in London, of a woman, with a strangely deformed face, resembling that of a pig, who is possessed of a large fortune, and we suppose wants all the comforts and conveniences incident to her sex and station. We ourselves, unwittingly put in an advertisement from a young woman, offering herself to be her companion; and

yesterday morning, a fellow (with a calf's head, we suppose) transmitted to us another advertisement, attended by a one pound note, offering himself to be her husband. We have put his offer in the fire, and shall send his money to some charity, thinking it a pity that such a fool should have any. Our rural friends hardly know what idiots London contains . . .

Despite such condemnation, London newspapers continued to publish reports about the Pig-faced Lady of Manchester Square for several more months.

———— • ————

The Worst Actor in England

☞ *28 Montagu Square*
Map: D

One of the best-known eccentrics of Regency England was Robert Coates – better known as 'Romeo' Coates – the son of a wealthy sugar-plantation owner in the West Indies. Coates proclaimed himself the finest actor of his generation, and when he failed to make a living on the stage he simply financed his own performances.

Coates was renowned for forgetting his lines and inventing new ones – and indeed whole new scenes – off the top of his head. He would also repeat his favourite scenes up to three or four times during a performance and had a particular penchant for reprising melodramatic deaths.

Coates was convinced that many of the classics required improvement and that he was the man to do it. He was especially inventive with *Romeo and Juliet*, in which he appeared many times. When he played Romeo on one occasion he tried to prise Capulet's tomb open with a crowbar; on another he took a pinch of snuff during the balcony scene and proceeded to offer it round to the audience; and in Romeo's death scene he famously used his hat as a pillow and cleaned the stage with his handkerchief before lying down. Eventually no actress would appear opposite him as Juliet.

Coates, however, seems not to have taken himself too seriously and all his performances were made to raise money for charitable causes. He called himself 'the Celebrated Philanthropic Amateur'. After 1816 his popularity waned and, finding it increasingly difficult to lease premises, his theatrical career came to an end.

Off the stage, Coates was as entertaining as he was on it. He was famous for wearing clothes covered with diamond buttons and for dressing in fur no matter what the weather. His motto, 'While I live, I'll crow', was emblazoned along with a heraldic cockerel on his seashell-shaped carriage, often seen outside his house in Montagu Square.

Romeo Coates's death was suitably dramatic. He died in February 1848 after being knocked over by a hansom cab whilst leaving a performance at the Theatre Royal in Drury Lane.

———————— • ————————

Heart Attacks and Parking Tickets

☞ *Great Cumberland Place*
Map: E

On 19 September 1960 traffic wardens made their first appearance on London's streets. There were forty of them and, dressed in their military-style uniforms, they were empowered by the Metropolitan Police to issue fines of £2 to offending motorists.

The unlucky recipient of the first ever ticket was Dr Thomas Creighton, who had parked his Ford Popular outside the Cumberland Hotel while he answered an emergency call to a heart-attack victim there. The public outcry that followed forced the authorities to back down and let Dr Creighton off the fine, but the incident dealt a blow to the reputation of traffic wardens from which they have never recovered.

———— • ————

The Monkey and the Hunchback

☞ *Portman Mansions, Porter Street*
MAP: F

The attractive blocks of Victorian flats named Portman Mansions, built in the 1890s, stand on the corner of Chiltern Street and Porter Street, which runs east from Baker Street, parallel to Marylebone Road.

If you look up to the top of the buildings you will see two unexpected statues. One, at the corner with Chiltern Street, is of a monkey with a long tail, while the other, at the western end of the blocks on the opposite side of the road, is of a hunchback. Strangely, these statues were never part of the original plans of the building, but appear to have materialized overnight sometime in the summer of 1935.

Breast Implants, Bull Sperm and the Dawn Chorus

☞ *200 Baker Street*
Map: G

Tucked around the side of Baker Street station, and appropriately just across the street from Sherlock Holmes's fictitious residence at number 221b, is London Underground's fabled Lost Property Office. It opened in 1933 and collects, collates and returns all the lost items left on the tube.

Some of the stranger items to have been handed in include:

- false eyes
- replacement limbs
- 125 kg of sultanas
- a Chinese typewriter
- breast implants
- a six-foot teddy bear
- a stuffed eagle
- a fourteen-foot boat
- a grandfather clock
- a bishop's crook
- a garden slide
- a canister of bull sperm
- an urn of ashes
- three dead bats in a container
- a stuffed puffer fish
- a vasectomy kit
- two human skulls in a bag

The absent-minded professor who left this last item on the tube was eventually reunited with his possessions, and the breast implants, forgotten on the Central Line by a courier who was taking them to a Harley Street clinic, are now walking around somewhere, their owner unaware of how well travelled her chest is.

The office's box of false teeth regularly receives new additions, and people do come to try to find their missing dentures. One pensioner collected a set, only to return later, spit them out on the front desk and complain that they might have looked familiar but did not fit.

Money, of course, is frequently lost, but among the office's biggest finds was a briefcase containing £10,000 in cash. Its owner, an elderly man to whom it was eventually returned, apparently did not trust banks.

A canister of bull sperm must rank among the most bizarre and least savoury items to turn up. It was disposed of with some haste.

The Lost Property Office also has its own version of the dawn chorus, when between 7 and 9 a.m. all the alarms on the thousands of lost mobiles start to ring and bleep.

MAYFAIR

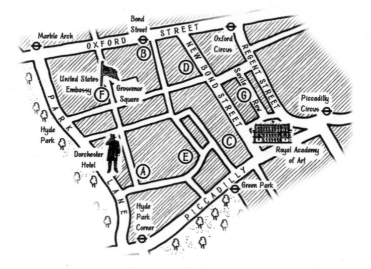

The Secret of Audley Square

☞ *2 Audley Square*
MAP: *A*

Audley Square, which runs off South Audley Street in the heart of Mayfair, has played an unusual role in the history of European diplomatic relations.

At the height of the Cold War in the 1950s and 1960s, the lamppost outside number 2 was used as a message drop by the spies of the Russian Secret Service. If you look closely, you will see a little trapdoor in its side. It was here that the spies would deposit and collect their coded messages.

A rather odd postscript to this was that, when casting for the James Bond film *Dr No*, producers Cubby Broccoli and Harry Saltzman had their office next door at number 3.

——————— • ———————

The Peabody Estate Fences

☞ *Gilbert Street*
MAP: *B*

After the Second World War a large number of metal stretchers, which had been stored in readiness for the expected deluge of civilian casualties, had to be disposed of.

There was much debate about how to get rid of this huge amount of ironware, but the problem was solved with the need to build more blocks of flats to house the unfortunate people whose homes had been bombed.

It was decided that the stretchers should be used as railings in the new Peabody Estates – social housing estates being built around London.

Although many of the fences have since been removed or replaced, coming out of the south side of Bond Street Underground station you can still see some of these original railings surrounding the block of flats opposite.

_____ • _____

The Naturist and the Cowbell

☞ *26 Dover Street*
MAP: C

It was here in the 1840s that Joseph Henry Blake, third Lord Wallscourt, stayed during his many visits to London. He was a pioneering Irish socialist and was much taken with the concept of cooperative communes. He tried to implement socialist theories on his own estate in Ardfry, County Galway, with mixed success. Alas, it is not for his socialist principles that he is lauded today, but for his advocacy of naturism.

He was convinced that the only way to achieve constant good health was to be naked between the hours of 10 a.m. and 4 p.m. – a theory that he put into practice daily. His long-suffering wife insisted that he wear a cowbell around his neck in order to warn the servants of his approach.

Sadly, the intended benefits of nudity did not work. Lord Wallscourt died of cholera in 1849 at the age of only fifty-one.

Hendrix and Handel

☞ *23 and 25 Brook Street*
MAP: *D*

In this row of elegant Georgian properties, two adjoining houses each proudly bear an English Heritage Blue Plaque. The great composer George Frideric Handel lived at 25 Brook Street from 1723 until his death in 1759. And next door, at number 23, the plaque announces that this was where Jimi Hendrix, the wild man of the electric guitar, resided in an upstairs flat from 1968 until 1969.

It appears that Handel paid rent of £60 a year for his whole house in the 1730s and it was the first private home he had in London. Hendrix and his girlfriend, Kathy Etchingham, paid £30 a week for their attic flat. Hendrix wrote in 1968: 'This is my first real home of my own.'

On hearing about the Handel connection, Hendrix went out and bought records of *Messiah* and the *Water Music*. It is claimed by some that you can make out pieces of Handel in the thunderous guitar chords of Hendrix's later recordings.

———— • ————

The Only Running Footman

☞ *5 Charles Street*
MAP: *E*

Dating from 1749, this pub was once called the Running Horse. It was a popular meeting place for the many footmen employed in this wealthy part of London, one of whom, when he left service, bought it and renamed it after himself. It is properly called the I *Am* the Only Running Footman.

Although these days we tend to think of footmen as house servants, their original role was to run alongside their master's coach to make sure it avoided any obstacles or pedestrians in the road and to pay any tolls. They were also employed to fetch and carry messages. The household accounts of King Charles I, dating from the early seventeenth century, record that a footman was paid two shillings (ten pence today) to run from London to Hampton Court on an errand.

It seems that often a footman was as much for show as for use, because as well as proving that he was quick on his feet, part of the usual selection procedure was that the candidate must possess well-turned legs that could be shown off by the traditional footman's dress of stockings worn below knee-breeches.

Employment as a footman was a very coveted and lucrative position. In the mid-eighteenth century the annual salary was £7, with full board and a smart uniform, but with tips (known then as 'vails') his earnings could rise to £40 a year (about £60,000 today).

Such was their reputation for speed that the nobility would often arrange races between their men, gambling on the outcome. On 3 July 1663 Samuel Pepys recorded in his diary:

> The town talk this day is of nothing but the great foot-race run this day on Banstead Downs, between Lee, the Duke of Richmond's footman, and a tyler, a famous runner. And Lee hath beat him; though the King and Duke of York and all men almost did bet three or four to one upon the tyler's head.

The Duke of Queensberry, who was renowned for his love of a wager (see pages 53–4), was determined to employ the quickest footmen. On one occasion, though, he was beaten at his own game, as reported in *The Survey of London*:

> The duke was in the habit of trying the pace of candidates for his service by seeing how they could run up and down Piccadilly,

watching and timing them from his balcony. They put on a livery before the trial. On one occasion, a candidate presented himself, dressed, and ran. At the conclusion of his performance he stood before the balcony. 'You will do very well for me,' said the duke. 'And your livery will do very well for me,' replied the man, and promptly ran away with it.

Over time, as roads in the city were widened and improved, there was less need for running footmen and their role gradually changed to assisting the butler, and other household duties.

————— • —————

The Duke of Westminster's American Embassy

☞ *Grosvenor Square*
MAP: F

The first United States Embassy in London was established in 1785 and was situated in Great Cumberland Place. Ever since that time, however, there has been an American presence in Grosvenor Square, as John Adams, the first US Ambassador to the Court of St James (as he was known), lived at number 9, on the corner of Brook Street and Duke Street. The embassy itself had several other locations around central London before moving to 1 Grosvenor Square in 1938. During the Second World War General Eisenhower had his headquarters at number 20 and the US Navy's European office was also in the square.

Then in the late 1950s the Duke of Westminster, whose family, the Grosvenors, is the biggest landowner in this part of London, agreed to allow the Americans to demolish buildings on the west side of the square to put up the building we see today.

Thus began one of the most bizarre land negotiations the capital has ever seen.

Wherever in the world the Americans had an ambassador, they had always first bought the land and then built their embassy. Assuming this would be the case in England, they asked the Duke of Westminster how much he would sell the site for.

What they did not know was that the duke's wealth was based on the fact that the Grosvenors lease all their properties and land. The freeholds are never sold.

When the Americans were told that they could not buy the site, they were furious and petitioned Parliament to force the duke to sell. Questions were asked in the House, but the duke would not back down. He did, however, come up with a marvellous compromise.

If the Americans were prepared to return to his family all the land in the United States stolen from them after the American War of Independence, then he would allow them to buy their site in Grosvenor Square.

The Americans knew when they were beaten: they would have had to give the duke most of Maine and New York. So they backed down and accepted his offer of a 999-year lease.

And that is why the American Embassy in London is the only one in the world that does not belong to the United States.

Margaret Thompson, Snuff Junkie

☞ *8 Boyle Street*
MAP: G

This was the home of Mrs Margaret Thompson, perhaps the greatest known devotee of snuff, who died here in 1776.

According to the terms of her will, she was buried in a coffin filled with unwashed snuff handkerchiefs, and her body was sprinkled with a large quantity of best Scottish snuff. The six most fervent snuff-takers in the parish acted as pall-bearers and they wore snuff-coloured beaver hats instead of black.

In return for a bequest of snuff, Mrs Thompson's servants were instructed to walk in front of the funeral procession throwing snuff on the ground and into the watching crowd. And throughout the day, snuff was to be distributed to all comers from the door of her house here on Boyle Street.

Even the vicar conducting the funeral ceremony was invited to take as much snuff as he desired during the service and five guineas' worth was provided for him to do just that.

PICCADILLY

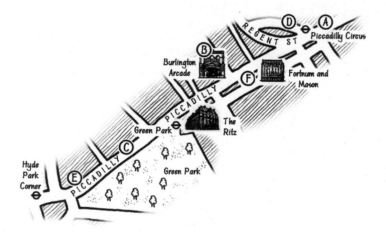

The Coventry Street Vampire

☞ *Coventry Street*
MAP: A

This short street in the heart of London's West End may seem an unlikely location for supernatural activity, but it was here that a series of alleged vampire attacks took place on the same April day in 1922.

At 6 a.m. on 16 April a clerk making his way along Coventry Street to work fell to the ground unconscious. When he woke up he found himself in Charing Cross Hospital, where the doctors who were treating him told him he appeared to have been stabbed in the neck by some kind of thin tube. The man, however, insisted that he had been set upon by an invisible force, which had leapt upon him from the shadows and bitten his neck, sucking out his blood.

As the day progressed, two other victims were brought into the same hospital from exactly the same place on Coventry Street, both of them displaying identical wounds to the first patient.

The police could come up with no explanation. The press, however, lost no time in picking up and spreading rumours that a vampire-like attacker was prowling the streets. A story circulated that the police had hired a vampire hunter, who succeeded in tracking down the perpetrator and stabbing him through the heart with a stake. The corpse was reportedly interred in a vault at Highgate Cemetery.

What really happened remains still a mystery, as there were no more attacks after that day.

No Whistling or Opening Umbrellas

☞ *Burlington Arcade*
MAP: *B*

Burlington Arcade – the upmarket shopping precinct connecting Piccadilly with Burlington Gardens – was the creation in 1819 of Lord George Cavendish of Burlington House (now the home of the Royal Academy) on Piccadilly. It is said that he conceived the innovative covered format out of a desire to prevent Regency rowdies from throwing oyster shells into his garden and to allow his wife and friends to shop in safety.

Lord George then decided to employ members of his family regiment, the 10th Hussars, as 'beadles', charged with enforcing a strict code of behaviour on customers at the arcade. Regulations included no whistling, singing, playing of musical instruments, running, carrying of large parcels or opening of umbrellas, and no babies' prams. The rules are still in force today.

The reason behind the ban on whistling was that, when the arcade first opened, the rooms above the shops were used by prostitutes, who also kept a lookout on behalf of the pickpockets milling amongst the crowds below. From their vantage point, the girls would whistle a warning when they saw the police approaching.

There is, however, one man to whom this rule does not apply. Paul McCartney was caught whistling and was reprimanded by one of the beadles, who was obviously not a Beatles fan, whilst strolling through the arcade in the late 1980s. He later received an apology from the embarrassed beadles, with written permission to whistle in the arcade at any time.

In the nineteenth century the beadles, who were stationed at either end of the arcade, had a leather armchair at the entrance on which to sit whilst keeping an eye on visitors. It was also the beadle's job to ring a hand-bell to tell the shops to close.

Wearing their distinctive gold-braided top hats and frockcoats, the world's smallest police force still patrols the arcade today.

Piccadilly and the End of the World

☞ *Piccadilly*
MAP: C

In 1750 London was disturbed by two earth tremors severe enough to bring down a pair of old houses and a number of chimneys. The first occurred on 8 February and the second four weeks later, on 8 March. Fears grew that after another month a third earthquake would strike.

There was much alarm, and some apothecaries did brisk trade in pills for the warding off of earthquakes. More dramatically, a former member of the Life Guards (subsequently sent to Bedlam) was summoned to court in order to answer charges of blasphemy after walking up and down Piccadilly shouting out that the world would end on 8 April.

Despite his arrest, on the evening of 7 April there was mass panic. In the days leading up to the expected disaster a huge number of Londoners had made plans to escape the city, and lodgings had been taken as far out as Windsor. But Piccadilly was so choked with traffic that many got no further than Hyde Park, where, according to Horace Walpole, 'women made earthquake gowns, that is, warm gowns to sit out of doors all night', whilst men played cards, awaiting the apocalypse that never came.

The Cross-dressing Colonel

☞ *Regent Palace Hotel, Glasshouse Street*
Map: D

At this Piccadilly hotel on the morning of 28 February 1929, Colonel Leslie Victor Barker was arrested for failing to appear at a bankruptcy hearing. The handsome ex-army officer went with the police quite willingly.

When he was remanded to Brixton Prison to await his trial date, the prison doctor gave the new arrival a routine medical examination and much to his surprise discovered that Colonel Barker was a woman!

The revelation came as a total shock to Barker's wife, Elfrida. In an interview, she stated that she was 'dazed, stunned! In our six years of married life I never once suspected that dear Victor was a woman too!' She had always believed, she said, that their lack of a love life was due to her 'husband's' war wounds.

As police set about interviewing Colonel Barker (who had been quickly moved to Holloway) the truth began to come out. Valerie Barker had been born in Jersey in 1895 and had a typical middle-class upbringing. She grew from being a tomboyish girl into a strapping woman, 'nearly 6ft high and powerfully built'.

In 1914, aged nineteen, Valerie volunteered to serve as a nurse and ambulance driver during the First World War, and four years later she married an Australian officer, Harold Arkell-Smith, but the marriage soon failed and they divorced. A few years later, in 1923, and now known as 'Colonel' Barker, she married Elfrida Emma Howard.

The colonel then became involved in the British Organization of Fascists and taught fencing and boxing to the teenage recruits before taking a job as a desk clerk in the Regent Palace Hotel.

When the trial started, it became the sensation of the day and every detail was eagerly followed. For many people it was the first time they had heard the word 'transvestite'.

Valerie Barker was eventually sentenced to nine months in Holloway Prison, though incarceration appears not to have dampened her zeal for cross-dressing and on her release she quickly went back to being Leslie Barker. After drifting between different fairgrounds as an attraction for a while, she eventually faded into obscurity and died in 1960.

———————— • ————————

The Duke of Queensberry, Wacky Bets and Cow's Milk

☞ *138 Piccadilly*
MAP: E

In the second half of the eighteenth century, an age famed for the profligate behaviour of its society rakes, none was more notorious than William Douglas, third Earl of March and later fourth Duke of Queensberry, who lived here on Piccadilly. An incorrigible womanizer, he was equally well known for his dissipation and gambling.

Not only did he like to bet at cards, but he was also obsessed with proposing wagers on the most far-fetched things. He placed one of his most famous in 1747 upon his election to the gentlemen's club White's. The event became known as 'the race against time', for Queensberry bet that a four-wheeled carriage drawn by four horses could travel a course of nineteen miles in less than an hour.

Such a feat was laughed off as impossible, in part due to the poor quality of the roads and in part because the carriages of the time weighed so much and were very difficult to manoeuvre – so whoever accepted the wager must have felt fairly sure of winning. The duke, however, had no intention of losing. He designed and commissioned a special lightweight carriage, in which every possible ounce was saved. Whalebone and silk were used to make the traces and harnesses, and the finished vehicle weighed just over two hundred pounds – a fraction of an ordinary coach.

When the race took place on Newmarket Heath on 29 August, the nineteen miles were covered in just fifty-three minutes and twenty-seven seconds.

Queensberry dedicated the same energy and inventiveness to other wagers into which he entered. On one occasion he claimed that it was possible for a letter to travel fifty miles within one hour. When the bet was accepted, he hired twenty cricketers to stand twenty feet apart in a circle, then he inserted the letter into a cricket ball and had them throw it to each other as fast as they could. Needless to say, he won that one too.

The duke's pursuit of young women was equally ruthless. If a pretty girl caught his attention, he would dispatch his manservant, Jack Radford, to take a note to her. Amazingly, this method was successful, for he never seemed to be short of attractive female companions. His determination knew no bounds. In 1752, having become enamoured of Miss Frances Pelham, he bought number 17 Arlington Street, the house next door to hers. Horrified, her brother, the Hon. Henry Pelham, barred Queensberry from calling, but the duke was undeterred. He simply had a bow window installed in number 17 through which he could continue to gaze upon the fair Miss Pelham.

His advancing years did little to mellow 'Old Q', as he was known, and he whiled away his days on the balcony of his house at 138 Piccadilly, ogling the ladies going by. In the summer of 1803 the poet Leigh Hunt observed him sitting there and 'wondered at the longevity of his dissipation and the prosperity of his worthlessness'.

A further eccentricity of Queensberry's was his habit of bathing in gallons of cow's milk, which he firmly believed would help revitalize him. It was said that Londoners of the time were extremely wary of drinking milk, afraid that the duke might have sold it on after his baths.

Napoleon's Carriage and the Wonders of Nature

☞ *170–173 Piccadilly*
MAP: F

On this site opposite Burlington House stood the Egyptian Hall, which opened in 1812. With a façade in the style of an ancient Egyptian temple, it was commissioned by the naturalist and antiquarian William Bullock and originally housed his collection, which included historical objects and curiosities brought back from the South Seas by Captain Cook.

In 1816, an exhibition of Napoleonic relics, including Napoleon's carriage taken at Waterloo, drew crowds of thousands and made the Egyptian Hall one of the most popular venues in London.

Later in the nineteenth century the Victorians grew very fond of the 'wonders of nature', and the hall hosted many attractions, including the famous conjoined twins Chang and Eng Bunker from Siam (Thailand today), whose nationality gave us the term 'Siamese' twins, and the American dwarf General Tom Thumb. Other sensations were 'the Hairy Woman', whose eyebrows covered her forehead, as well as a Dutch boy who displayed the words 'Deus Meus' ('My God') and 'Elohim' ('Mighty One') on each iris.

Towards the end of the nineteenth century the hall became famous for its magic productions, most notably those of J. N. Maskelyne and his son Nevil, who developed acts that still intrigue audiences today, such as levitation and sawing a woman in half.

The hall continued as an exhibition venue until 1895 when it was demolished. This extraordinary flight of fancy was replaced with an office block called Egyptian House.

ST JAMES'S

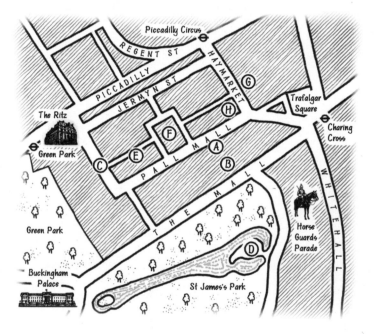

The Athenaeum Stones

☞ *107 Pall Mall*
MAP: *A*

The Athenaeum Club in Pall Mall is one of the country's most famous gentlemen's clubs. Since its foundation in 1824, its distinguished membership has included Charles Dickens, Charles Darwin, Sir Arthur Conan Doyle, Winston Churchill and many other influential people from the worlds of politics and the arts.

However, none of its members has received quite the same treatment from the club as the Duke of Wellington, the 'Iron Duke', who defeated Napoleon at the Battle of Waterloo in 1815.

Following a request from Wellington, the Athenaeum ordered the creation of a pair of granite stones to allow the duke, in his old age, to mount and dismount his horse outside the club. They are still there today, positioned on the kerb facing the front door, where they have been lying relatively unnoticed for the past 170 years.

On the stones is a rusty plaque: 'This horseblock was erected by desire of the Duke of Wellington 1830'.

Whether other members of the club were also permitted to take advantage of the duke's steps is unknown.

The Only Nazi Memorial in London

☞ *9 Carlton House Terrace*
MAP: B

There is just one memorial to a Nazi in London, and that is to a dog. Named Giro, he was a terrier owned and much loved by Dr Leopold von Hoesch, German Ambassador to London from 1932 to 1936. When Giro died in February 1934, Hoesch buried him in the grounds of the German Embassy, in what was formerly the front garden to number 9 Carlton House Terrace. It is now a small space between the Duke of York Steps and the former embassy's garage ramp, but the tombstone can still be seen, bearing the inscription 'Giro: ein treuer Begleiter!' ('Giro: a true companion!').

Hoesch himself died in office in 1936 and was accorded a full diplomatic funeral with a nineteen-gun salute in St James's Park.

Numbers 8 and 9 Carlton House Terrace served as the German Embassy in London before the outbreak of the Second World War. The Nazi architect Albert Speer oversaw the buildings' renovation and it is claimed that Mussolini donated the Italian marble used for the staircase.

When the Nazis left following the start of war in 1939, the former embassy became a department of the War Office. Most of the Nazi interior was removed, but apparently one room still has a design of swastikas on its floor.

Today, numbers 6–9 Carlton House Terrace are the headquarters of the Royal Society.

The Unfortunate Case of the Colonel and the World's First Traffic Island

☞ *St James's Street*
MAP: C

In 1864 a Colonel Pierpoint designed the world's first ever traffic island, which he had built in St James's Street so that he could cross the street safely to reach his club, the Carlton Club.

Unfortunately, while showing some admiring friends his latest creation, he tripped over the island and was knocked down and killed by a passing cab.

—————— • ——————

The Governor of Duck Island

☞ *St James's Park*
MAP: D

Duck Island, on the lake in St James's Park, has a rather strange story to tell.

During the reign of Charles II, relations between England and France were somewhat strained. So when the French soldier and writer Charles de Saint-Denis, seigneur de Saint-Evremond, was exiled from France for criticizing the country's all-powerful chief minister Cardinal Mazarin, his arrival in London meant the British monarch had a problem.

Saint-Evremond was extremely well connected and a very popular figure in London. Unfortunately, he was also very low on funds and was hoping for employment at the royal court. This caused a dilemma, because while King Charles certainly did not want to offend the French government, neither did he want to upset Saint-Evremond.

The solution he came up with was a novel one. He appointed Saint-Evremond governor of Duck Island, with no duties and a pension of £350, which in today's money equals £45,000 a year.

This delighted the Frenchman, even though he had no idea where Duck Island was. It also met with the approval of the French ambassador, who knew exactly where it was.

So Saint-Evremond, still blissfully unaware of the provenance of his title, lived out the rest of his days as governor of Duck Island. He was by all accounts in later life a dreadful glutton and died in 1703 after eating too many grapes.

The governorship was extinguished with our grape-eating friend, but in 1733 Queen Caroline, consort of George II, revived it in order to bestow it upon one of her favourites, a poet appropriately named Stephen Duck.

Duck Island itself is still there, although it is no longer an island but joined to the rest of the park.

————— • —————

The Most Exclusive Dance in England

☞ *28 King Street*
MAP: *E*

In late eighteenth-century England, if you wanted to be on the 'A-list', then Almack's Assembly Rooms was the place to be seen. At the time London clubs were usually a strictly male preserve and Almack's was one of the very few that accepted carefully selected lady members as well as gentlemen. So it was here that the chosen ladies could dance with the most eligible bachelors in England; even just to be admitted implied you had arrived as a member of the social élite. It was the pinnacle of aspiration for a young lady on the hunt for a husband.

Balls were held once a week during the summer, on a Wednesday evening, and entrance was via a blue voucher at a cost of ten guineas. It was very difficult to obtain a voucher, however, as the rather formidable members of the Almack's all-woman committee were extremely particular about the credentials of all applicants. In order to keep out 'undesirables', they insisted on good breeding. But not even being a member of the nobility guaranteed acceptance, for only about half of all applicants were ever granted vouchers.

The patronesses of Almack's guarded entry to the club like Valkyries prepared to do battle, 'their smiles and frowns consigning men and women to happiness or despair'. The Duke of Wellington was once famously turned away because he had committed the unforgivable faux pas of arriving seven minutes late and wearing trousers rather than knee-breeches.

The duke was not the only person of rank who was censured. A report dated 1765 states: 'The Duchess of Bedford was first blackballed, but is now since admitted, the Duchesses of Grafton and of Marlborough are also chosen. Also Lady Holderness, Lady Rochford are blackballed, as is Lord March.'

Captain R. H. Gronow wrote in 1814 that:

> **At the present time one can hardly conceive the importance which was attached to getting admission to Almack's, the seventh heaven of the fashionable world. Of the three hundred officers of the Foot Guards, not more than half a dozen were honoured with vouchers of admission to this exclusive temple of the beau monde . . .**

Eventually Almack's lost its exclusivity as the rules were gradually relaxed when the original patronesses died. The club did continue, though, until 1871, when it finally shut its doors.

The premises were then sold, but continued as a club under the name of Willis's Rooms, after the new owner.

The building was damaged during the bombing of London in 1940 and completely destroyed in 1944. The site is now occupied by offices (Almack House), but bears a brass plaque commemorating the existence of the famous assembly rooms.

———— • ————

Man Arrested for Wearing a Shiny Structure

☞ *St James's*
MAP: F

On 17 February 1797, a man named James Hetherington took an evening stroll through St James's with a new type of hat on his head.

Hetherington was a haberdasher and this was the first appearance in London of a top hat. But his walk did not go to plan. According to witnesses, the sight of a man with such a strangely disfigured head caused an enormous commotion. A large and somewhat hysterical crowd gathered, pushing and jostling to the extent that one child had his arm broken and Hetherington was arrested on a charge of disturbing the peace.

The police officer who apprehended him testified in court that 'Hetherington had such a tall and shiny construction on his head that it must have terrified nervous people. The sight of this structure was so overstated that various women fainted, children began to cry and dogs began to bark.'

The law proved as suspicious as the mob and the unfortunate Mr Hetherington was given a fine.

In its report of the incident, *The Times* commented: 'Hetherington's hat points to a significant advance in the transformation of dress. Sooner or later, everyone will accept this headwear. We believe both the court and the police made a mistake here.'

The Times, of course, was right. Within a very few years the top hat was the height of fashion.

—————— • ——————

Mr Bisset's Amazing Cats' Opera

☞ *Haymarket Theatre, Haymarket*
MAP: G

In the mid-eighteenth century, entrepreneurial Londoners were constantly thinking of new forms of entertainment. A certain Mr Bisset – originally a shoemaker from Perthshire – had some initial success with showing a monkey, whom he trained to ride a pony and dance with a dog.

But this was not particularly unusual for the time, and Bisset realized that to be truly successful he would need to present something no one had tried before. He decided upon his master plan: he was going to train cats.

According to Richard Mercier's *Anthologia Hibernica*, published in 1793, 'He taught those domestic tigers to strike their paws in such directions on the dulcimer, as to produce several regular tunes, having music-books before them, and squalling at the same time in different keys or tones, first, second, and third, by way of concert.'

In 1758 Bisset entered into partnership with the famous showman William Pinchbeck and leased the Haymarket Theatre for the premiere of *Bisset's Amazing Cats' Opera*. The spectacle opened with such entertainments as cats strumming dulcimers and mewing, one monkey dancing with a dog and another playing the barrel organ, and a hare that walked on its back legs whilst beating a drum. The show became enormously popular and earned Bisset and Pinchbeck a small fortune.

This success convinced Bisset of his ability to train any animal. He went on to teach six turkeys to perform a country dance, canaries and sparrows to distinguish the time of day – but it seems even his extraordinary skills failed when he tried to train a goldfish.

Ho Chi Minh, Pastry Chef Revolutionary

☞ *80 Haymarket*
MAP: *H*

In 1913, before becoming president of the Democratic Republic of Vietnam, the young Ho Chi Minh took a job in the kitchens of the Carlton Hotel. Auguste Escoffier, often regarded as the patron saint of chefs, was in charge of the kitchens at that time and seems to have taken the young revolutionary under his wing.

Ho Chi Minh's first job at the hotel was as a dish-washer. It is said that whenever he found large pieces of meat that had been left untouched on diners' plates, rather than throwing them out he would put them on a clean plate and send them back to the kitchen.

When Escoffier saw him doing this, he asked, 'Why didn't you throw these into the bins like others do?' Ho Chi Minh answered, 'These things shouldn't be thrown away. You could give them to the poor.' 'My dear young friend,' Escoffier replied, 'please listen to me! Leave your revolutionary ideas aside for now, and I will teach you the art of cooking.'

Before long, Ho Chi Minh was promoted and began to learn the art of fine French patisserie from Escoffier himself. He apparently enjoyed the work and demonstrated considerable talent; Escoffier is said to have believed that Ho Chi Minh could have had a promising career in the world of haute cuisine – but the young Vietnamese had other ambitions.

In its day the Carlton was one of the most famous hotels in the world. Unfortunately it existed for only forty years. It opened in 1899 and was completely destroyed during the London Blitz in early 1940. It is now the site of New Zealand House, where a plaque commemorating Ho Chi Minh's time here can be seen.

WESTMINSTER

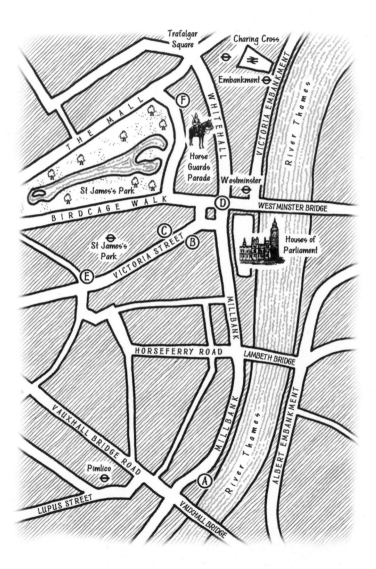

The Tate and Transportation

☞ *Millbank*

MAP: A

In 1889 Henry Tate, the sugar magnate and philanthropist, gave his distinguished collection of sixty-five contemporary paintings to the nation, with the proviso that a gallery would be created to display them properly for the public to enjoy. He also donated £80,000 towards the costs of such a building. The National Gallery of British Art was opened on 21 July 1897, on the site of the old Millbank Prison; its name was changed to the Tate Gallery in 1932 when it was expanded to house the national collection of modern art; and in 2000, when Tate Modern opened at Bankside, it became Tate Britain.

The prison itself had been built as the National Penitentiary and was used as a holding facility for convicts due for transportation to Australia. It was designed at the end of the eighteenth century by the philosopher Jeremy Bentham as a 'Panopticon' – a building in which a watchman could continually observe all the inmates from one position, although they themselves would be unable to tell whether or not they were being watched. Much to Bentham's annoyance, though, the Panopticon design was never used.

A large circular bollard stands by the river in front of the gallery, with the inscription: 'Near this site stood Millbank Prison which was opened in 1816 and closed in 1890. This buttress stood at the head of the river steps from which, until 1867, prisoners sentenced to transportation embarked on their journey to Australia.'

The phrase 'down under' is said to be derived from a nearby tunnel through which the convicts were walked in chains down to the river. Depending on their crime, prisoners could be given the choice of receiving a five- to ten-year jail sentence instead of transportation.

Among the many to be sent to Australia – and perhaps the unluckiest of them all – was Isaac Solomon, a convicted pickpocket who was said to be the inspiration for Fagin in Charles Dickens's *Oliver Twist*. In 1827 he managed to escape while being taken to Newgate Prison. He fled the country to New York, but then travelled on to Tasmania when he discovered that his wife had been transported there for crimes of her own. Alas, upon arrival he was re-arrested, shipped home to London, re-tried, re-convicted and sentenced to be transported for fourteen years . . . back to Tasmania.

--- • ---

Buried Upright in Westminster Abbey

☞ *Westminster Abbey*
MAP: B

Ben Jonson (1572–1637), the famous dramatist, poet and contemporary of Shakespeare, is the only person buried in an upright position in Westminster Abbey.

There are various explanations for why he was interred in this unusual fashion. It has been suggested that he wanted to be ready for Judgement Day, but the most popular story is that he asked King Charles I if he would grant him eighteen square inches of land anywhere of his choosing in England. The king agreed, but urged Jonson to accept a larger piece of land. The poet, however, refused the offer, saying that this amount would serve his purpose. When King Charles granted his request, Jonson asked for his eighteen square inches to be in Westminster Abbey and on his death he was buried here, in the north aisle of the nave, standing upright in order to fit into the tiny plot. A stone was erected to mark his grave, bearing the simple but misspelt inscription 'O Rare Ben Johnson'.

Nearly a hundred years after his death, a memorial was erected to Jonson in Poets' Corner, but those who wished to see him remembered perpetuated the misspelling of his name and once again he appears as Johnson, rather than Jonson.

The First Human Cannonball

☞ *Methodist Central Hall Westminster, Tothill Street*
MAP: C

On this site, facing Westminster Abbey, stood the Royal Aquarium and Winter Garden, designed in classical style by Alfred Bedborough and opened in 1876 as a grand Victorian entertainment venue. It housed palm trees, restaurants, an art gallery, an orchestra, a skating rink, and also smoking and reading rooms. A variety of sea creatures were displayed, but the aquarium itself suffered from plumbing difficulties and the place became much more famous for the exciting performances staged here than for its fish.

Between 1877 and 1884, the renowned Canadian showman and tightrope-walker known as the Great Farini (real name William Leonard Hunt) produced many extravagant spectacles in the Royal Aquarium. Most famously, in 1877 a fourteen-year-old girl called Rossa Matilda Richter, but better known as Zazel, was launched through the air from a device designed by Farini, thus becoming the first ever human cannonball. The 'cannon' was basically a long tube fitted with springs, and the perceived lighting of the wick and subsequent 'bang' were all part of the ruse. The poor girl, who was barely five feet tall and weighed less than six stone, was frequently sent flying thirty feet or more. Protests were raised over the danger of this and other acts, and for a while the venue risked losing its licence, but nevertheless crowds flocked to see the performances.

By the 1890s the Aquarium's reputation had become less respectable and it was known as a place where ladies of poor character went in search of male companions. Eventually this became too much for Victorian propriety and the venue was closed in 1899. It was demolished four years later.

In 1905 the land was acquired for the building of Methodist Central Hall Westminster, which still occupies the site.

The World's First Exploding Traffic Lights

☞ *Houses of Parliament*
MAP: D

The world's first traffic lights were installed in front of the Houses of Parliament, at the junction of George Street and Bridge Street, in 1868, in an attempt to regulate the traffic of horse-drawn carriages on London's increasingly crowded streets.

Designed by John Peake Knight, a railway signals engineer, it was a simple construction, intended to imitate the gestures of a traffic policeman. A green-painted iron pillar, standing twenty-four feet high, weighing five tons and adorned with gilding, was fitted with manually operated movable arms. If the arms stuck straight out at 90 degrees to the post, traffic was obliged to stop; if the arms were at 45 degrees, vehicles could proceed but must 'be cautious'. So that the arms could still be seen at night, red and green gas lights were added.

The new traffic signal enjoyed immediate but short-lived success. Three weeks after it was erected, on 2 January 1869, a leaking gas valve caused the pillar to explode, leaving the policeman who was operating the signal with severe burns. The traffic lights were condemned as hazardous and removed immediately.

It was to be sixty years before London saw its next traffic lights, when a modern three-colour version, pioneered in the United States, was installed at the junction of Piccadilly and St James's Street in 1929.

The Smuttiest Windows in London

☞ *Albert Tavern, 52 Victoria Street*
MAP: E

Etched into the frosted windows of this pub is a surprising image: nothing less than the willy of – presumably – Prince Albert, consort of Queen Victoria and embodiment of moral rectitude, after whom the establishment is named. Two odd circular marks on the royal member point towards the (probably apocryphal) position of the so-called Prince Albert piercing, and the organ is depicted at the moment of *petit mal*.

The prince's private parts and their stream of 'pollution' are cunningly woven into a background of leaves and scrolls. But despite the camouflage, this unusual window still wins a place amongst the smuttiest in London.

———————— • ————————

The Secret Service Gardener

☞ *The Admiralty Citadel, Horse Guards Road*
MAP: F

Just to the north of Horse Guards Parade there is a slightly non-descript, ivy-clad, dark red building, originally constructed to protect the Admiralty from bombs during the Second World War.

This odd building does not seem to appear in any London guide. At the time, the press were forbidden to mention it and great lengths were taken to make sure the building was undetectable, particularly from the air. It was designed to withstand bombing, but the War Cabinet was still concerned about camouflaging it from above: a problem that was solved, rather innovatively, by growing grass on top of it.

This led to a rather strange ritual which continues to this day. During the summer months a man with a lawnmower presents himself to the officials within the building and, after satisfying them of his credentials, is allowed to enter. He then exits through an upstairs window on to a set of steps that lead to the roof, mows the lawn, carries his mower and a black plastic bag full of grass cuttings back downstairs, then leaves the building.

TRAFALGAR SQUARE

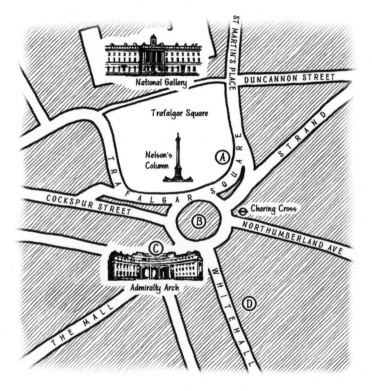

National Gallery

ST MARTIN'S PLACE

DUNCANNON STREET

Trafalgar Square

STRAND

Nelson's Column

Ⓐ

TRAFALGAR SQUARE

COCKSPUR STREET

Ⓑ

Charing Cross

NORTHUMBERLAND AVE

Ⓒ

Admiralty Arch

WHITEHALL

Ⓓ

THE MALL

The Smallest Police Station in Britain

☞ *Trafalgar Square*
MAP: *A*

Cunningly located at the south-east corner of Trafalgar Square is Britain's smallest police station. It was constructed in 1926 so that the Metropolitan Police could monitor demonstrations in Trafalgar Square, which was traditionally a centre for protests. But it would be easy to pass it by without noticing it, as it was actually created inside an ornamental stone lamppost that stood at the edge of the square.

Once it had been hollowed out, a set of narrow windows was installed to allow the occupant to see out over Trafalgar Square. It also had a dedicated phone line back to Scotland Yard in case of emergency. The ornamental light fitting would flash, alerting other nearby policemen whenever the phone was picked up.

Sadly, the box is no longer used by the police. Since the 1970s it has instead as acted as a broom cupboard for Westminster Council cleaners.

The Exact Centre of London

☞ *Charles I Statue, Trafalgar Square*
MAP: B

Wherever the destination, the actual point for measuring distances to and from London is the site of the original Charing Cross – now occupied by a statue of Charles I on horseback – at the top of Whitehall, on the junction of the Strand and Cockspur Street. This is regarded as the exact centre of London.

The reason Charing Cross assumed this importance is not because of its central location, however, but because of its role in a funeral procession. In 1290 King Edward I was in Scotland awaiting the arrival of his queen, Eleanor of Castile, but during her journey north she was taken ill with a fever and died at Harby, near Lincoln.

Protocol demanded that she be taken back to Westminster Abbey for burial, a journey which lasted twelve days, and the grief-stricken king decided that a memorial cross should be erected at each stopping point on her funeral procession.

The twelve sites were: Lincoln, Grantham, Stamford, Geddington, Hardingstone, Stony Stratford, Woburn, Dunstable, St Albans, Waltham, Cheapside (formerly West Cheap) and finally the village of Charing just outside Westminster. Only three of the original crosses remain – at Geddington, Hardingstone and Waltham.

The Charing Cross was destroyed during the Civil War. A replica, made in 1863, currently stands outside the station that bears its name, a few hundred yards away. The statue of Charles I, which was erected in 1633, now marks the 'centre of London' and if you visit today you will see a plaque on the wall confirming this.

Distances from London:

- Manchester 184 miles
- Paris 257 miles
- Glasgow 389 miles

- Geneva 539 miles
- Rome 1,118 miles
- New York 3,358 miles

- Beijing 5,055 miles
- Los Angeles 5,455 miles
- Rio de Janeiro 5,762 miles
- Cape Town 6,003 miles

- Bangkok 5,931 miles
- Sydney 10,500 miles
- The moon 240,000 miles

———— · ————

Lord Nelson's Spare Nose

☞ *The Mall*
MAP: C

On the left-hand inner wall of Admiralty Arch, you will see a small nose protruding from the wall. This is said to be Lord Nelson's second nose, just in case the first one on his statue in Trafalgar Square falls off or is dislodged by a pigeon.

The nose is about seven feet off the ground, sitting at waist height for anyone riding through the arch on a horse. It is said that the Horse Guards always touch it for luck as they ride by.

Alas, there is a far more sensible explanation for its existence. It was placed there relatively recently by artist Rick Buckley as part of a campaign against the 'Big Brother' society and in particular the widespread introduction of CCTV cameras. In 1997, Buckley stuck thirty-five casts of his own nose to landmarks around London, including the National Gallery, Tate Britain and the South Bank Centre. Some were detected and removed within hours or weeks, but ten survive to this day. Apart from the one in Admiralty Arch, six remain in and around Soho: in Covent Garden piazza, Bateman Street, Dean Street (at Quo Vadis), Denmark Street, off the Strand and near the Trocadero. Two noses at the Hayward Gallery and one on a South Bank walkway also survive.

Mr Speaker and the Pavements

☞ *Craig's Court*
MAP: D

Walking through the streets of London in the eighteenth century was extremely hazardous. Not only were the thoroughfares very narrow, but the roadway occupied the whole space between the buildings on each side. Pedestrians, horses and carriages all jostled for space, and anyone on foot could easily be crushed against a wall.

It took the unlikely figure of the Speaker of the House of Commons, Arthur Onslow, to solve the problem. One day in the spring of 1761 Mr Speaker Onslow set off to visit the Earl of Harrington in his house just off Craig's Court in Whitehall. A narrow alleyway led to the house and, as Onslow's carriage passed through it, the wheels jammed against the houses on either side. It was stuck so tightly that the coach's doors couldn't be opened and Onslow became trapped inside. After many failed attempts to move the vehicle, the red-faced and by all accounts extremely angry Speaker was rescued by bystanders who cut a hole in the roof of the carriage and pulled him out.

Determined to do something about the problem, Onslow forced a Bill through Parliament compelling every householder to pay for a row of kerbstones to be put in front of their property to mark a boundary showing the limit of the roadway for traffic. And from this the pavement was born, and finally pedestrians were able to walk in relative safety.

THE STRAND

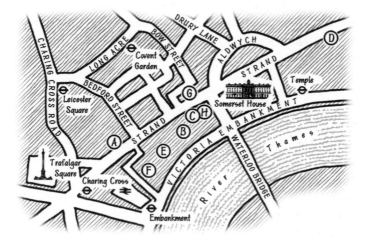

Killed by a Falling Stone Penis

☞ *Zimbabwe House, 429 the Strand*
MAP: *A*

In 1938 an unnamed pedestrian was struck on the head and subsequently killed by a stone phallus falling from one of the statues adorning what had once been the headquarters of the British Medical Association.

The eight-foot nude figure was one of a series of eighteen by the sculptor Jacob Epstein, positioned high up on the façade of the building on its completion in 1908. They represent the *Ages of Man* and were Epstein's first important work in London. When they were put in place, the sight of huge, beautifully sculpted genitals was too much for many Edwardian sensibilities and caused a good deal of outrage in certain quarters. Father Bernard Vaughan, a member of the National Vigilance Society, raged in the *Evening Standard* that: 'As a Christian citizen in a Christian City, I claim the right to say that I object most emphatically to such indecent statuary being thrust upon my view.'

Not everyone felt that way. People flocked into London for precisely that reason. Artists and critics were also very supportive of Epstein, and the BMA decided to stand firm against pressure to remove the sculptures.

In 1938 the building was bought by the Rhodesian High Commission and work was begun to clean the grime-stained façade. Unfortunately the hoses used to wash down the stone appear to have weakened the willy of one of the statues and it was only a matter of time before it fell off – alas on to the head of our unfortunate passer-by.

Shortly after taking residence, the Rhodesian High Commission emasculated all the remaining statues.

Today, the building is the location of the Embassy of Zimbabwe.

Farting Lane

☞ *Carting Lane*
MAP: B

On Carting Lane, which runs down from the Strand towards Embankment on the west side of the five-star Savoy Hotel, is a Webb Patent Sewer Gas Lamp, invented in the late nineteenth century by Joseph Webb. The underground sewer system was badly ventilated in those days, and the lamp was designed to reduce health hazards by drawing off germs and bad smells, and to lessen the risk of explosion from the build-up of gases. It was also seen as a low-cost, low-maintenance way to keep London lit up at night.

The lamp was connected to the city gas supply, and heat from two constantly burning mantles positioned in a small dome in the roof of the sewer drew the methane from the sewers upwards, then diverted it into the lamp on the street above. The lamp remained lit twenty-four hours a day, seven days a week, powered at least partly by the bowel movements of the guests staying at the nearby Savoy.

It didn't take long for witty locals to rename the road 'Farting Lane'.

In 1953 a reversing lorry hit the lamp and almost destroyed it, but it was restored and is still in operation today. It appears to be the last remaining methane-powered lamp in London.

The Savoy's Lucky Cat

☞ *Savoy Hotel, the Strand*
MAP: C

For more than a hundred years London's Savoy Hotel has maintained the superstition that it is unlucky for thirteen to sit down to dinner. If there is a table of thirteen in any of the hotel's restaurants, then a wooden lucky black cat named Kaspar is given a setting alongside the diners, wearing a white napkin around his neck and with a saucer of milk placed in front of him.

The tradition dates from 1898, following a banquet thrown by the wealthy South African diamond magnate Woolf Joel for fourteen people, including himself. At the last minute, one of the invitees was unable to come, reducing the number present to thirteen. One of the guests reminded everyone that this was considered unlucky, and that same diner later went on to predict that the first person to leave the table that evening would be the first to die. Joel laughed at the idea and he himself left first.

Several weeks later, the news came that Joel had been shot dead in his office in Johannesburg.

The hotel, shocked by the news and worried that their reputation might be damaged by association, from then on adopted the practice of placing a member of staff on every 'unlucky' table of thirteen. But this was unpopular with diners, who disliked the intrusion on their privacy, so in 1927 the designer Basil Ionides – who was employed to refurbish the interior of the Savoy Theatre – created a two-foot-high sculpture in the form of a lucky black cat to act as the fourteenth guest.

When his company is not required at the dining table, Kaspar sits in a display case in the hotel foyer. He has now also been immortalized in print, in the book *Kaspar, Prince of Cats* by the children's writer Michael Morpurgo, who was Writer in Residence at the Savoy in 2007.

———— • ————

Lady Pedal Power

☞ *222 the Strand*
MAP: D

Now a branch of Lloyds Bank, this building was once home to one of the first air-conditioned restaurants in London. It opened in 1883 and was in business for only three years, during which time a pair of ladies recruited from a local cycling club would pedal a tandem bicycle in the basement which would power a giant pair of bellows, forcing air into the ground-floor dining area above.

The owner of the restaurant, a Mr Cedric Browne, was an extremely fat man who was in the habit of taking a brandy or three whilst counting the takings at the end of each day. One evening, however, he leant back in his chair; the leg snapped and he fell to the ground, breaking his neck.

The restaurant closed shortly afterwards.

Dr Graham and his Amazing Celestial Bed

☞ *Adelphi Terrace*
MAP: E

The late eighteenth century was a time when quacks and the practice of bogus medicine abounded. None was more notorious than Dr James Graham, an early sex therapist and advocate of 'electrical cures'. He was also one of the most successful, with scores of wealthy devotees.

James Graham was born in Edinburgh in 1745 and studied medicine at the university in the city, but failed to complete his degree. He travelled to America, where he became fascinated by Benjamin Franklin's electrical experiments and began to develop his own theories about the benefits of electricity in curing all sorts of medical conditions. He became a firm believer in shock therapy, which was then in its infancy, and wrote many articles on the subject.

Upon his return to Britain, Graham set up residence in London. He began converting a large house in the Adelphi into the magnificent 'Temple of Health'. When it opened its doors in August 1779 it became an immediate success and attracted a number of wealthy clients from the upper echelons of society, particularly ladies, on whom the good-looking and charming Dr Graham made a profound impression.

The venue was a clinic and also a showcase for his theories: clients, all of whom paid a two-guinea entrance fee, could buy medicines and consult with Graham, who lectured here and distributed his publications on marriage guidance; they could also enjoy music therapy and inspect his electrical equipment. Adorning the classical interior, scantily dressed as 'Goddesses of Health', were ladies who embodied Graham's ideas of perfection. Emma Lyons, the future Lady Hamilton, was one of them.

Following the popularity of this venture, in 1781 Graham expanded his business into Schomberg House in Pall Mall, where he launched his Temple of Hymen, which again offered music, drama, talks and therapies, but with a clearly erotic flavour. A vast and unmistakably phallic electrical conductor dominated the drawing room, attracting much comment. Eleven feet long, it rested suggestively on two glistening globes.

Most intriguing of all, however, was the famous Celestial Bed. It could be rented for £50 a night, and Graham advertised that anyone who slept on it would be cured of impotence or sterility. It was enormous – twelve feet long by nine feet wide – and its mattress was stuffed with 'sweet new wheat or oat straw', rose leaves, lavender, herbs and, to guarantee vigour, hair from the tails of English stallions. It could be tilted to different angles, and over it hung a huge mirror. But its most unique feature was the electricity that sparked from the bedhead into the air around, 'calculated to give the necessary degree of strength and exertion to the nerves'. Like a form of eighteenth-century Viagra, it promised to deliver a sublime ecstasy. It seems, however, that Graham had misjudged the public's appetite for such things. When the novelty had worn off, he found himself in debt and reluctantly closed the doors a mere three years after opening. He moved back to Edinburgh, where he became increasingly eccentric. He began preaching, founded his own church and towards the end of his life was signing his letters 'O.W.L.' – Oh Wonderful Love. He was seen taking off all his clothes in the street to give them to the poor, and for some time he was ordered to be detained in his own home as a lunatic.

Meanwhile Graham's experiments with health continued. One of them was earth-bathing, in which his patients were buried up to their necks in order for the earth to 'cleanse' their bodies. Indeed, so convinced was he of its efficacy that he delivered several lectures while buried in this manner. His final theory was that fasting would lengthen his life, and in 1794 he died of starvation in the process of proving it.

Celebrity Street

☞ *Buckingham Street*

Map: F

Buckingham Street, which runs up from Embankment towards the Strand, is arguably London's greatest celebrity street, boasting a rich history of famous residents. The list includes:

No. 9

Peg Woffington (1720–1760) lived here 1755–1757

A celebrated beauty and famous Irish actress, Woffington had a string of affairs with famous men of the day, including the renowned actor David Garrick, Edward Bligh (second Earl of Darnley) and MP Charles Hanbury Williams. In 1757, she was playing the part of Rosalind in *As You Like It* when she collapsed on stage. This was her last performance, and she died from a wasting illness less than three years later.

No. 10

David Hume (1711–1776) lived here in 1766

The Scottish philosopher, economist and historian David Hume is often regarded as one of the most important philosophers ever to write in English, although he was apparently extremely argumentative. Samuel Johnson wrote of him, 'I would rather leave the room than find myself in the same company.' During his time in Buckingham Street he was visited by the French philosopher Jean Jacques Rousseau, to whom Hume referred as his 'pupil'. Rousseau seems to have taken an instant dislike to London and, after a number of quarrels with Hume, packed his bags and left after a stay of only two weeks.

Henri Rousseau (1844–1910)

Post-Impressionist painter and friend of Picasso, Rousseau in his best-known paintings depicts wonderfully detailed jungle scenes, even though he never saw a jungle in his life. His stay at No. 10 was probably quite brief.

Thomas Russell Crampton (1816–1888) lived here 1849–1850

A railway engineer best known for the laying in 1851 of the first practical submarine cable between Dover and Calais, Crampton was also responsible for many improvements to locomotives and for various other inventions.

Samuel Pepys (1633–1703) lived here 1685–1687

Best known for his diary, and in particular his description of the Great Fire of London in 1666, Pepys first stayed at number 12 with his friend William Hewer in 1679 after being released from the Tower of London, where he had been held on a charge of spying. In 1685 he himself became the householder here. By this time he was Secretary to the Admiralty, and he continued to live here until 1687, when he moved next door to the larger number 14 (see below).

Humphry Davy (1778–1829) lived here 1824–1826

The chemist and inventor of the Davy Lamp, which allowed miners to work safely in the presence of flammable gases, was not at all popular with his neighbours during his tenure here, as he turned the cellar into a laboratory where he would perform experiments involving foul-smelling gases in order to investigate the corrosion of ships' hulls.

Samuel Pepys (1633–1703) lived here 1687–1701

Pepys moved here from number 12 (see above).

Sir Robert Harley (1661–1724) lived here 1701–1714

Some historians insist Harley, who was Lord Treasurer to Queen Anne, was really Britain's first ever prime minister, predating Sir Robert Walpole. Both Jonathan Swift, author of *Gulliver's Travels*, and William Penn, founder of Pennsylvania, stayed here with him on several occasions. During his tenure at number 14 he was Speaker of the House of Commons (from 1701 until 1705), Chancellor of the Exchequer in 1710 and Lord Treasurer in 1711.

William Etty (1787–1849) lived here 1826–1849

Born in Yorkshire, Etty upset London society with his massive paintings of mythological nudes. One canvas, *The Combat*, was over ten feet high and thirteen feet in breadth, causing the *London Magazine* to comment on 'The biggest breasts in Christendom'. While he was living in Buckingham Street, *The Combat* was exhibited at the Royal Academy.

The painter and antiquarian J. T. Smith, in his *Book for a Rainy Day*, published in 1829, requested his readers to 'look up at the three upper balconied Windows of that mass of building on the south west corner of Buckingham Street. Those and the two adjoining Westminster, give light to chambers occupied by that truly epic historical painter, and most excellent man, Etty, the Royal Academician, who has fitted up the balconied room with engravings after pictures of the three great masters; Raphael, Nicholas Poussin, and Rubens. The other two windows illumine his painting room, in which his mind and colours resplendently shine.'

No. 14

Clarkson Stanfield (1793–1867) lived here 1826–1831

Concurrently with William Etty on the top floor, a lower part of number 14 was occupied for some years by Clarkson Stanfield, a Victorian landscape artist whose most famous work, *The Battle of Navarino*, was painted here in 1828. He also pioneered the 'moving diorama', an early-nineteenth-century form of cinema, which consisted of huge paintings that unfolded on rollers like scrolls. They were accompanied by sound and lighting effects and the show sometimes included stage props and singers. Unfortunately, whilst Stanfield was preparing for a performance in 1830, the apparatus caught fire in his living room, badly damaging the house.

No. 15

Peter the Great (1672–1725) lived here in 1698

Tsar Peter I of Russia lived here on his frequent visits to London. He was by all accounts a very odd-looking man. At six feet eight inches he was extremely tall for the time, but had very small hands and feet, very narrow shoulders and a tiny head. Despite these handicaps he still managed to father fourteen children.

Henry Fielding (1707–1754) lived here in 1735

The author of *Tom Jones*, still regarded as one of the greatest comic novels in the English language, Fielding was in residence at number 15 while producing his farce *An Old Man Taught Wisdom*; the play's dedication is dated 'Buckingham Street, February 12th'. Fielding is also well known as the founder in 1749 of the Bow Street Runners, London's first police force.

Charles Dickens (1812–1870) lived here in 1834

The great Victorian novelist lodged at number 15 while working as a reporter for the *Morning Chronicle*. He drew on his time living here in his novel *David Copperfield*, in which he describes the view of the Thames from his window and the activities of his drunken landlady, Mrs Crupp. Dickens knew the area well, as he had worked near here as a twelve-year-old, putting labels on bottles in a boot-blacking factory that was located under the site of the present-day Charing Cross station.

In his will, Dickens stipulated that no monuments were to be erected to commemorate his life, which is why London has no statue of one of its greatest writers.

No. 21

Samuel Taylor Coleridge (1772–1834) lived here in 1799

One of the foremost Romantic poets, author of *The Rime of the Ancient Mariner* and 'Kubla Khan', Coleridge was perhaps the first rock-'n'-roll poet, known for his opium and laudanum habit. His translation of Friedrich Schiller's *Wallenstein* was written whilst he lived here.

No. 22

Napoleon Bonaparte (1769–1821) lived here in 1791

As a young officer, Napoleon lived here during the autumn of 1791, supposedly in order to spread the ideals of the French Revolution to England. It obviously did not work, as a few years later most of Europe was at war with him.

The Elephant of the Strand

☞ the Strand

MAP: G

Before London Zoo opened in Regent's Park in 1828, there were menageries all over the city. The owner of one such place was a Mr Edward Cross, who owned and managed a collection of animals on the upper floors of the Exeter Exchange on the north side of the Strand in the early nineteenth century. Among the exhibits was a five-ton Indian elephant called Chunee. The animal came into Cross's hands around 1810 at a cost of 900 guineas and was an instant attraction. Lord Byron was so taken with him on a visit to the menagerie that he offered to buy him, but he was not for sale.

The elephant was extremely well behaved, though as he grew older he became subject to short fits of ferocity. To keep these in check he was doped, but this did not always reduce his violence.

In March 1826, after he had been captive for many years, Chunee finally made a bid for freedom during his weekly walk along the Strand with one of his keepers. He broke free and in the ensuing rampage the keeper was killed. Chunee was eventually recaptured and returned to the menagerie, but Cross was by now extremely concerned about the animal's growing aggression and decided he should be put down.

The first attempt was made by poisoning his food, but Chunee refused to eat it, so Cross called in the troops from nearby Somerset House to dispatch him. Upon the command of his trusted remaining keeper, the elephant obediently knelt down in front of the firing squad. But no one had realized how tough an elephant's hide was, and despite the soldiers firing 152 bullets into him, he still didn't die. Poor Chunee was finally killed with a sword-thrust from his keeper.

There was widespread outrage at the manner of the animal's

death, but Edward Cross continued to make a profit from Chunee by charging the public to watch him being dissected – which droves of people turned up to see.

Mr Kessler's Birthday Party

☞ *Savoy Hotel, the Strand*
MAP: H

The Savoy Hotel has had its fair share of eccentric guests and for a time in the early twentieth century the management seems to have been very happy to accommodate their whims.

In June 1905, the American financier George A. Kessler wanted to celebrate his birthday by throwing an extravagant party at the hotel. Following his instructions, the management arranged to have the courtyard flooded and filled with swans, then surrounded with twelve thousand fresh carnations and four thousand lamps, all against a five-hundred-foot canvas backdrop of

Venice. Kessler dined with his guests on a large, silk-lined gondola moored in the centre. After dinner the world-famous Italian tenor Enrico Caruso sang an aria and a baby elephant appeared with a five-foot birthday cake strapped to its back. Unfortunately, the blue dye that had been used to colour the water proved fatal to the swans which presumably put something of a dampener on proceedings.

A few years later two Americans who were staying at the Savoy had a heated argument over whether it would be possible to cast a fly, using a salmon rod, from the roof of the hotel into the Thames below. A wager was agreed and the next Sunday morning, tied to a chimney on the hotel roof and with the help of a policeman who stopped the traffic below, one of them proved that it was indeed possible and won the bet.

Other notable eccentrics include a Canadian guest who took potshots with his twelve-bore shotgun at geese flying towards Green Park, and the great violinist Jascha Heifetz, who had bagpipe lessons on the roof.

EMBANKMENT

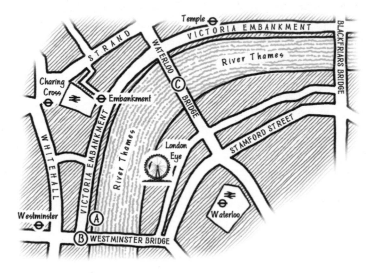

The Lions' Head Early-warning System

☞ *Victoria and Albert Embankments*
MAP: A

Long before the construction of the Thames Barrier, there was a rather lovely, not particularly scientific way of alerting London to the danger of flooding.

Along both sides of the Thames Embankment there are rows and rows of lions' heads with mooring rings in their mouths, sculpted between 1868 and 1870 when the Embankment was being built. At first sight, they appear to have no real practical use, for they are too far down the parapet to allow anyone to disembark safely.

In fact, they are a unique part of London's flood-warning system and are behind the saying: 'When the lions drink, London will sink'. The story goes that policemen walking alongside the Thames were told to keep an eye on the lions, because once the water reached the top of their heads, there was a real danger of flooding.

There still is a Metropolitan Police Standing Order that if this occurs all London Underground stations are to be closed immediately.

Boozed-up Bismarck

☞ *An unknown bench near Westminster Bridge*
Map: B

When Otto Edward Leopold von Bismarck, the Chancellor of Germany, came to England in 1885 on a state visit, he was subjected to the usual succession of meetings, functions and formal dinners. However, he apparently expressed an interest in visiting a London brewery, so this was speedily arranged and he was taken to the now defunct Barclay Brewery in Southwark.

At the end of his tour, he was asked if he would care to sample the company's strongest beer. Bismarck was delighted by the idea and was given a half-gallon flagon full of frothy ale. Etiquette normally demanded that the visitor would just take a sip and hand it back. Bismarck, assuming that it was all for him, drank the lot.

The manager of the brewery then joked to the chancellor that very few men had ever drunk two of the half-gallon tankards. Bismarck, aware that German honour was at stake, insisted on a refill and promptly drank that as well.

Still walking in a straight line, Bismarck left the brewery to thunderous applause and got into his carriage, which then left for Westminster.

Just after passing over Westminster Bridge, the carriage stopped. The most powerful man in Germany got out and lurched towards one of the benches by the side of the river. He told his staff that he intended to sleep it off, leaving strict instructions to wake him in one hour.

So while members of the Foreign Office waited patiently in their carriages, Germany's most powerful statesman fell fast asleep on the bench.

One hour later, he awoke and, seemingly refreshed, got back into his carriage and set off back to Whitehall to continue his diplomatic meetings.

The Bridge That Went to War

☞ *Waterloo Bridge*
MAP: C

In 1932 the decision was made to rebuild Waterloo Bridge, but while the new one was being constructed it would mean no access across the Thames. The solution was to erect a temporary metal bridge alongside the old one. This was a 'Rennie' bridge – the kind of steel structure in which army engineers specialize.

The new Waterloo Bridge was known as the 'Ladies Bridge', as much of its construction took place during the Second World War, when most men were in uniform and women had to be called upon to help complete it.

When the bridge was finished in 1942, the temporary affair was dismantled and stored away, seemingly forgotten.

But cometh the hour, cometh the bridge. In June 1944 the Allies were on the advance across Europe and there were only a few serviceable bridges over the Rhine. So out of mothballs came the temporary Waterloo Bridge, which was sent across the Channel and overland to the Rhine, where it was re-erected.

So across 'Waterloo Bridge' rumbled the tanks and armour of the Allies into Nazi Germany. When hostilities ceased it was packed up once again, only to be stolen from an army camp in Belgium. Despite considerable efforts, it was never found – a casualty of war.

SOUTHWARK
AND WATERLOO

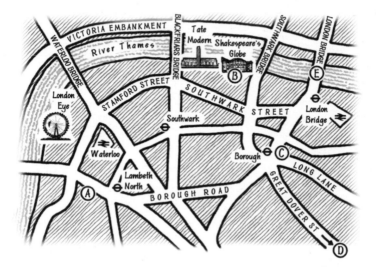

The Stiffs Express

☞ *121 Westminster Bridge Road*
MAP: A

This was once the site of London's strangest railway station – the terminus of the Necropolis Railway, which operated between 1854 and 1941.

In the mid-nineteenth century, cemetery spaces in London were becoming increasingly limited due to the rapid increase in population and the legacy of the cholera outbreaks of recent years. So in an effort to find a solution, the ever-inventive Victorians – in this case a man named Richard Bourn – started the rather spookily named Necropolis Railway Company. A station was first of all set up in York Street, opposite Waterloo, from where trains would transport the London dead to Brookwood Cemetery in Surrey. When Waterloo was expanded at the turn of the twentieth century, the Necropolis line had to be relocated to allow more room for regular train services, so a new terminus was opened here in Westminster Bridge Road in 1902.

The railway was divided both by class and by religion, with separate Anglican and Nonconformist sections and first-, second- and third-class tickets for each. These class divisions didn't just apply to the travelling mourners; they affected the style in which the deceased travelled, with more ornate coffins and storage compartments for first class, whilst in third class the plain coffins were stacked up and crammed into a hearse carriage.

On arrival at the terminus, mourners would be led either to one of the dedicated first-class waiting rooms (for first- and second-class funerals) or to the communal third-class waiting room. The coffin would be discreetly unloaded from the hearse and sent to platform level by lift.

At its peak, fifty corpses a day were transported along this line.

One of the more notable bodies to be carried by the train was that of Friedrich Engels, the German socialist political theorist and philosopher, who died in London on 5 August 1895. Engels had expressed a wish to be cremated and for his ashes to be scattered at sea, but at the time there was no crematorium near London, so he was taken first to Brookwood, then on to Woking Crematorium.

By the 1930s London had more cemeteries and crematoria of its own, and the service had been reduced to two trains a week. During the Second World War the station was heavily damaged in an air raid, which brought the Necropolis Railway to a halt. The repair work was not seen as financially worthwhile, so at the end of the war the station building was sold as office space. The track to the cemetery was removed in 1947.

——————— • ———————

What a Load of Bollards!

☞ *New Globe Walk*
MAP: B

A distinctive feature of many of London's streets are the black iron bollards in the shape of cannon. These iconic fixtures date back to Britain's victory over the French at the Battle of Trafalgar in 1805, after which captured French ships were stripped of anything that could be put to use.

A large number of cannon were retrieved but, although these French guns were regarded as the best in the world in terms of accuracy and engineering, their size meant they were unsuitable for British ships. However, determined to make the most of such fine trophies, someone came up with the bright idea of recycling them as street bollards instead.

They caught on at once. The captured cannon were mainly located in the East End, both north and south of the river, but they were so popular that when they had all been put in place replicas were made and positioned much further afield.

After more than two centuries, the cannon-bollards are still being made today. Most of the original French ones have now been replaced, but some do remain. A fine example can be seen near the Globe Theatre on the South Bank.

———————   •   ———————

Why You Can Never Tell the Time in Bermondsey

☞ *St George the Martyr Church, Borough High Street*
Map: C

The clock in the tower of the church of St George the Martyr was made by George Clarke of Whitechapel in 1738 for the sum of £90. According to J. Ralph in his *Critical Review of the Public Buildings, Statues, and Ornaments, in and about London and Westminster* of 1743, the clock's four dials were painted 'in as good and handsome a manner as the Clock at Greenwich Church'.

To this day, though, three of the faces are painted white and illuminated at night, whilst one is black and remains unlit. The black one looks towards Bermondsey, whose parishioners refused to give any money to the church when it was being built.

Planning Permission and the Russian Tank

☞ *Corner of Mandela Way and Pages Walk*
MAP: D

Just off a side street on the Old Kent Road is a piece of wasteland, parked on which is a Russian tank.

The 35-ton vehicle is a T34 that was supposedly used against the Czechs in the Prague Spring uprising of 1968. It arrived in London in 1995 when it was used for the filming of a modern adaptation of *Richard III*, starring Sir Ian McKellen and Dame Maggie Smith. After filming, the tank was sold to Londoner Russell Gray, a property developer who was at the time very disgruntled because Southwark Council had refused him planning permission to build a house on the small piece of land he owned in Bermondsey.

When he had made his armoured purchase, he applied again for planning permission, this time to put a 'tank' on the site. Assuming he meant a water tank, the council granted it.

A magnet for graffiti artists, the tank has now attained a form of celebrity status and, in a fitting two-fingered salute, Russell Gray arranged for its gun to be aimed at the very same council offices that refused him his planning permission.

———— • ————

Doggett's Coat and Badge Race

☞ *London Bridge*
MAP: E

London is home to the oldest continually running sporting contest in the world. The winner receives the princely sum of £50, an orange-and-red tunic, a cap, knee-breeches and an engraved silver medallion the size of a dinner plate. Such are the spoils of the Doggett's Coat and Badge Race, a single-scull rowing contest that has been held on the River Thames for nearly three hundred years.

The race has always followed the same course, beginning at London Bridge and ending in Chelsea, where the event's founder, Thomas Doggett, lived (originally it went from the Swan Tavern at London Bridge to the Swan at Chelsea). As the race starts, the six competing scullers are followed by boats of spectators, including an umpire wearing a bicorn hat and a gold-braided admiral's coat.

Doggett's race harks back to a particularly colourful era in sport, when noblemen and working men alike were united by a shared love of betting. Thomas Doggett himself was not a sportsman. Born in Dublin, he achieved fame as a comic actor and impresario in London. (His most famous role seems to have been a character named Deputy Nincompoop.) In 1715, both to mark the occasion of George I's accession to the throne and to honour a young man who had ferried him home one rainswept night, Doggett announced a race for Thames Watermen who had just finished their apprenticeships, the winner of which would receive a coat and badge. Doggett also left a small annuity, along with the instruction that the race be held 'for ever'.

And so the race continues to this day. It is organized by the Fishmongers Company, a Livery Company of the City of London. It takes place on a Friday during July, with the precise date and time depending on the tides.

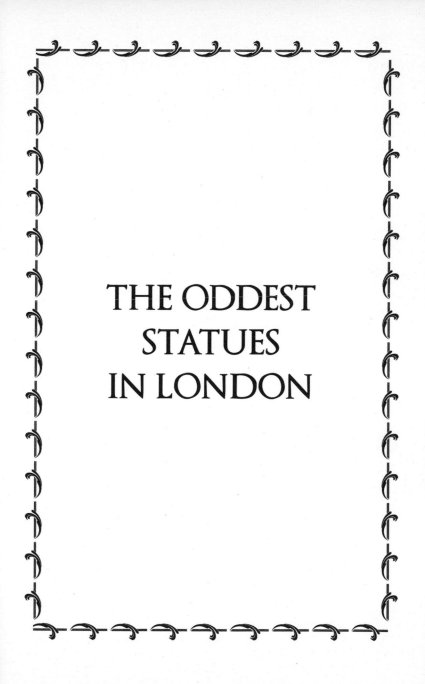

THE ODDEST
STATUES
IN LONDON

The Only Statue in England with a Squint

☞ *Fetter Lane*

In Fetter Lane stands possibly one of the most unflattering statues in England. Its subject is John Wilkes, the famous eighteenth-century radical and politician. He was elected Lord Mayor of London in 1774 and was instrumental in the introduction of parliamentary reform, arguing for yearly elections and the abolition of 'rotten boroughs'. Wilkes was also the first MP to propose universal suffrage in the Commons and during the American War of Independence he took the brave step of condemning British policy on America.

It appears that the sculptor did not bother to disguise poor old Wilkes's squint.

He was, despite his squint, a legendary womanizer. It was Wilkes who, when told by the Earl of Sandwich that he would die either of the pox or on the gallows, immediately replied, 'That depends, my lord, on whether I embrace your lordship's principles or your mistress.'

The Statue Left a Legacy

☞ *Fleet Street*

The figure of Elizabeth I that stands in the courtyard of the church of St Dunstan-in-the-West on Fleet Street is thought to be the oldest outdoor statue in London. It is the only statue of the queen that survives from her reign and was made in 1586. Originally it stood at one side of the old Ludgate. It survived the Great Fire of London and continued to adorn the restored Ludgate, but when that was demolished in 1760 it was moved to its present position at St Dunstan's.

In 1929 the statue came into an inheritance, when the suffragist Dame Millicent Fawcett, an admirer of Elizabeth I, left £700 in her will to pay for its upkeep.

A Little Piece of America

☞ *Trafalgar Square*

Outside the National Gallery in Trafalgar Square is a statue of George Washington, first president of the United States of America. Washington swore that he would never set foot in England, so in 1924, when the people of Virginia gave the statue to London as a gift, they also provided a pile of American soil to be placed underneath so that the president could keep his word.

———— • ————

Achilles' Penis –
the First Naked Man in London

☞ *Hyde Park*

The statue of Achilles near the south-eastern corner of Hyde Park was cast in 1822 from cannon taken in the Peninsular War and at Waterloo and presented by 'The Women of England' as a tribute to Arthur Wellesley, Duke of Wellington, who led Britain to victory in those conflicts. The statue is eighteen feet high, the largest in Hyde Park.

It was the very first statue of a naked man on public display in London and is anatomically correct in every way. In desperation to save blushes, a fig leaf was quickly added before the statue's unveiling.

The fig leaf has been broken off twice, in 1870 and 1961. If you look closely, you can see the join.

The Only Statue with an Umbrella

☞ *Waterlow Park*

Sir Sydney Hedley Waterlow was a Victorian philanthropist and politician. Today he is mainly remembered for donating his estate, Waterlow Park, which lies just south of Highgate in North London, to the public as 'a garden for the gardenless'.

His statue, at the entrance to the park, is said to be the only one in London showing a man with an umbrella.

--- • ---

The King and the Molehill

☞ *St James's Square*

Standing in St James's Square is a statue of William III. He is sitting majestically on a horse, much like the subjects of many other statues in London.

But on closer inspection, you can see a small molehill at the feet of his steed. The king was out riding one day in 1702 when his horse tripped on a molehill. William fell off and died soon afterwards from the pneumonia that developed from complications to his injuries.

William of Orange was the Protestant king brought to England from Holland to replace the Catholic King James II, who was forced to abdicate in 1688. To this day, all Jacobites traditionally toast 'the little gentleman in the black velvet waistcoat' – the mole that killed a king.

The Statue That Got Married

☞ *Smithfield*

In the central garden at Smithfield there is a statue of a young woman wearing a solid gold wedding ring.

In 1924 a ring was found by the market superintendent, who, after no one had claimed it, decided to solder it on to the statue's finger. As the statue was supposed to represent fertility, the churchgoing superintendent decided that she should be married.

SOHO

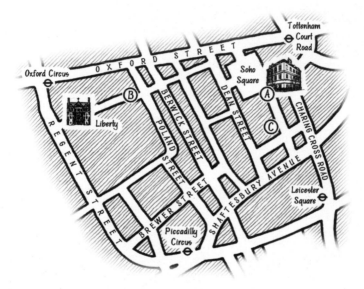

The House of Charity and its Coin Pipe

☞ *1 Greek Street*
MAP: *A*

Number 1 Greek Street, in Soho, is home to the House of St Barnabas, at one time known as the House of Charity, which has provided care and support for the homeless since its founding in 1846. The building itself dates from 1746 and was originally a private house, owned by a succession of wealthy families. In 1811 it became the offices of the Metropolitan Board of Works, whose chief engineer, Sir Joseph Bazalgette, was the genius behind London's sewage system. In 1862 the House of Charity moved here and the premises became one of the first hostels for the homeless in London, offering temporary accommodation, food and guidance to many thousands of people in need. From the end of the Second World War up until 2006 it was a hostel exclusively for women. The charity – which became the House of St Barnabas in 1961 – continues to this day, although the building is now used as an administrative office rather than as residential quarters. Charles Dickens knew Soho well and it is thought that he used the rooms and gardens of the House of St Barnabas as inspiration for the lodgings of Dr Manette and Lucie in *A Tale of Two Cities*. Fittingly, the road that leads round to the back of the house, formerly Rose Street, is now called Manette Street. Fixed to the railings at the front of the House of St Barnabas is a rather odd pipe with a slot for coin donations, which fall down the pipe to the alms box in the kitchen. People today still use it to donate to the charity and the accompanying plaque tells us that the Penny Chute has been accepting donations for over a hundred years.

The Meanest Man in England

☞ *Great Marlborough Street*

MAP: B

John Elwes, or 'Elwes the miser' as he was known, was the inspiration for the character Ebenezer Scrooge in Charles Dickens's *A Christmas Carol*. He was born John Meggott in 1714, the son of a successful and wealthy brewer named Robert Meggott, and Amy Elwes whose surname he would eventually adopt.

John's father died when the boy was four years old, leaving a fortune of £100,000 – around £9 million today. Despite her wealth, his widow is said to have died of starvation rather than spend anything.

Educated at Westminster and then in Switzerland, John initially gave little hint of the man he would become. He dressed well, spent money freely and moved in the most fashionable circles.

A change in his character came about, however, when he returned from Europe and was introduced to his uncle, Sir Harvey Elwes, who himself had a reputation for meanness and boasted that he lived on a mere £110 a year.

The young Elwes entertained hopes of inheriting Sir Harvey's wealth and endeavoured to please the old man. In the evenings he would sit with his uncle by a fire made with just one stick, while they gossiped about other people's extravagances and shared a single glass of wine. At bedtime they would creep upstairs in the dark to save the cost of a candle.

When Sir Harvey died in September 1763, John Elwes got his reward, as the old man left his nephew his entire fortune. He was now worth over £350,000, the equivalent of more than £36 million today.

By this point, though, Elwes had absorbed most of his uncle's habits. HIs clothes were ragged, and he wore a wig that a beggar had discarded in a hedge. He also had a coat that had gone green with age, which he had found blocking a hole in the wall of his house. Candles cost money, so he went to bed as soon as darkness fell, and he would walk in the rain rather than pay for a coach, then sit in his wet clothes because a fire to dry them meant buying wood. Even on the coldest day of winter Elwes was known to dine in an unheated room, saying that eating was 'exercise enough' to keep him warm. Although his house was expensively furnished, he refused to spend money on fresh food, instead eating meat so maggoty 'that it walked about his plate'. Once he is said to have eaten a moorhen that had been pulled from the river by a rat. He also railed against the birds that stole his hay for their nests.

When Elwes travelled, it was always on a run-down horse, which he would ride on the grass verge rather than the road in case its shoes wore out and needed replacing. His route would invariably be one that avoided turnpike tolls. Refreshment for the journey would consist of a hard-boiled egg and if he needed to sleep he would lie down under a hedge.

Perhaps surprisingly, John Elwes was elected on three occasions as Member of Parliament for Berkshire. Famously, his election expenses amounted to a mere eighteen pence and apparently he never spoke in Parliament. He was also a supporter of the architect Robert Adams and encouraged him in his plans for rebuilding London's West End. Elwes himself had inherited a number of houses around central London, to which he added as the years went by, eventually ending up with more than a hundred properties. In his later years he had no particular home of his own, but would shift around the city, staying for periods in whichever of his houses stood vacant.

Elwes's mania for frugality extended to his own family. He had two sons out of wedlock (because marriage cost money) and refused to pay for their education. 'Putting things into people's heads,' he explained, was 'the sure way to take money out of their pockets.'

In a last act of parsimony, when Elwes finally lay on his

deathbed he forced the lawyer who was drawing up his will to write by the light from the fireplace in order to save the cost of a candle. He died on 26 November 1789 in one of his untenanted houses in Great Marlborough Street.

Having lived on only £50 a year, Elwes's fortune had now increased to some £860,000 (£100 million today), which he left to his sons. As far as anyone knows, neither of them inherited their father's miserly ways.

---------- • ----------

Casanova's Parrot

☞ *47 Greek Street*
MAP: C

In 1763, 47 Greek Street was rented by a young Italian man – Giacomo Girolamo de Seingalt, better known to the world as Casanova.

Born in Venice in 1725, Casanova was the eldest son of two Venetian actors and (so he tells us) was a highly precocious, handsome and intelligent child. He went to the University of Padua at the age of twelve and graduated five years later with a degree in law, 'for which,' he said, he felt 'an unconquerable aversion'. Destined for a career in the Church, Casanova quickly realized that he found all kinds

of work boring. Instead, he decided to cultivate what he saw as his true vocation – the art of seduction.

With an expensive lifestyle and always on the lookout for new sources of income, Casanova travelled to England in 1763, hoping to sell his idea of a state lottery to English officials. Through his connections, he worked his way up to an audience with King George III, but to little avail.

As a means to find women, he advertised in a newspaper that he had an apartment to let to the 'right' person. He interviewed many young ladies, eventually choosing a beautiful young Swiss woman called Charpillon. Casanova seems to have become besotted with her. Soon he had installed her in an elegant house in Chelsea along with a number of her female relatives, including her mother.

But things did not turn out well. Before long the young lady had accused Casanova of grievous bodily harm, a crime which in those days could carry a life sentence. Casanova was imprisoned in Newgate and appeared before the magistrate Sir John Fielding (half-brother of the novelist Henry Fielding). He was found not guilty and acquitted.

Ever inventive, Casanova now came up with a novel form of revenge. A few days after his release he saw a parrot for sale. He bought it, hung its cage beside his bed and repeated the phrase: 'Charpillon is a bigger whore than her mother' over and over again until the parrot had learned it by heart. Casanova then paid a man to walk up and down the street where Charpillon lived, carrying the parrot in its cage while it shouted out its newly mastered phrase.

This exquisite form of torture went on for nearly two months until Charpillon and her mother packed their bags and left.

COVENT GARDEN

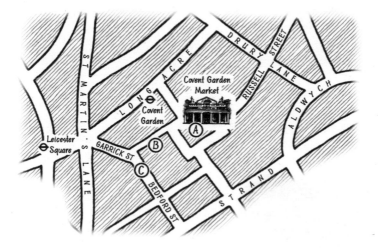

The Naughtiest Place in London

☞ *Covent Garden*
Map: *A*

These days Covent Garden is a safe, upmarket open-air shopping mall. But it was not always so.

In 1630, Inigo Jones built an elegant piazza on land that had once been the garden and orchard of the abbey at Westminster. This was London's first residential square and homes here were much sought after by the well-to-do. The area became even more desirable after the Great Fire destroyed much of the City of London.

The growth of the Covent Garden market, which opened in 1670, however, meant that soon the fashionable residents began to move further west and the area began to deteriorate. Also around this time Charles II reopened all the theatres in England, which had been closed in 1642 by the Puritans. The theatres brought rowdy crowds and attracted the criminal fraternity, so brawling and pickpocketing became rife, hastening the decline of the area.

By the late seventeenth century and on into the eighteenth, Covent Garden had earned a dreadful reputation as a warren of taverns, theatres, disreputable coffee shops and, of course, brothels, home to prostitutes like Long-Haired Mrs Spencer of Spitalfields and the delightfully named Fair Rosamund Sugarcunt, whose perfume was so intoxicating that lovesick suitors are said to have paid just to have their handkerchiefs impregnated under her pillow. By 1722 there were twenty-two gambling dens, fifty-six brothels and even a guide to over 170 Covent Garden prostitutes, listing their prices and services, and furnishing potential clients with descriptions and appraisals. Entitled *Harris's List of Covent Garden Ladies*, this directory was sold openly in the piazza and revised annually. For a long time it was attributed to a man named John Harris, but now it is believed to have been the work of a would-be poet called Samuel Derrick.

An unforgettable portrait of the riotous debauchery that so characterized Covent Garden at this time can be seen in the third scene of Hogarth's *Rake's Progress*, painted in 1733. The background here is the Rose Tavern, a notorious but very popular drinking place that stood at what is now the corner of Russell Street and Catherine Street and doubled as a brothel specializing in flagellation.

In 1754, however, the area's bawdy heyday came to an end when the author Henry Fielding (see also page 94) established the Bow Street Runners, the forerunner of the Metropolitan Police, on the edge of Covent Garden. With the criminals and prostitutes driven out, for the next two centuries it became a traditional working-class area.

In the midst of all the social changes, the district's one constant was Covent Garden's famous market. It continued to thrive throughout the eighteenth century and in 1830 Charles Fowler's new market hall was built, while the Flower Market opened its stalls in 1870. In 1974, however, the market moved to Nine Elms and the spirit of the place was transformed once more as it became the fashionable area we know today.

In its new character, Covent Garden nonetheless remains a centre of hustle and bustle. The sounds of the flower-sellers and the cries of the costermongers may now have been replaced with street performers and restaurants, but perhaps just a whiff of its days as the naughtiest place in London still lingers in the air.

The Essex Serpent and the Man Who Saved Christmas

☞ *The Essex Serpent, 6 King Street*
MAP: B

The alleged sighting in Essex in 1669 of a giant serpent gave this pub its name. The fearsome creature was described in a pamphlet as a 'Monstrous Serpent which hath divers times been seen at a Parish called Henham-on-the-Mount within four miles of Saffron Walden'.

The serpent was almost certainly a creation of wood covered in canvas and operated by a man inside. It is believed to have been built as a practical joke by the writer William Winstanley, who lived in the area and was well known for his pranks. It is more than likely that he wrote the pamphlet himself.

But it is not for his practical jokes that this gentleman is to be remembered and lauded, but as the man who saved Christmas.

Winstanley lived through the Civil War and the banning of Christmas by Cromwell's Puritans. They not only objected to the overindulgence, drunkenness and ribald revelry that accompanied Christmas week, but they also sought to abolish the festival (Christ's mass) as an unwanted remnant of Roman Catholicism. So they changed it to 'Christ tide' and any celebration was confined to just one day – of fasting and prayer.

So for sixteen long years, from 1644 to 1660, Britain was officially a country without Christmas.

When Charles II finally returned from exile in 1660, the Restoration of the monarchy meant that all the anti-Christmas legislation was repealed. But the country did not instantly return to the traditional feasting and celebration – it seems that over the years people had forgotten how to celebrate Christmas.

This is when William Winstanley stepped in.

Under the pen-name of Poor Robin Goodfellow, he wrote about the joy of Christmas. He came from a family of wealthy landowners and he tirelessly lobbied all of his class to set an example to their family, friends and tenants by opening their houses for feasting and entertainment, with log fires and decorations, feasting and games, and to make 'much mirth and mickle glee'.

For nearly forty years, right up to his death in 1698, he kept up his crusade to reclaim Christmas. His boundless enthusiasm gradually paid off and by the late 1680s festivities had started again.

———————— • ————————

Mrs Phillips' Preservatives

☞ *Bedford Street*
MAP: C

Constantia Phillips was a 'retired' courtesan who in 1732 opened the Green Canister, London's first sex shop, in Half Moon Street, which is now Bedford Street.

It appears that the enterprising Mrs Phillips catered for just about everything. She sold 'widow's comforters' in leather, ivory and wood, and customers could order bespoke flagellation machines. She also sold the Georgian equivalent of *Playboy*, with pamphlets on the 'education of young ladies' which were said to be alarmingly well illustrated.

But by far the most popular items of merchandise were her 'preservatives', or condoms.

Condoms, or 'cundums' as they were known, had been recorded in popular use since around 1500. The name 'cundum' first appeared in English in 1665, in a poem, 'A Panegyric upon Cundum', by the syphilitic literary genius John Wilmot, Earl of Rochester. For many years it was claimed that a certain Colonel Condom, the Royal Physician, had invented the device to put a stop to King Charles II's seemingly endless stream of bastard progeny, but sadly it has been found that the colonel never existed.

In the eighteenth century condoms were made from a sheep's intestine and in order to keep them elastic customers of the Green Canister were advised to soak them in water and squeeze them out before use. The standard length was between five and seven inches, and they were fastened in place with a coloured ribbon about the base.

Condoms appear to have been very popular with gentlemen. Casanova was a regular user, and while he was living in London his party piece was to blow them up like balloons to amuse his lady friends. The writer James Boswell became an avid fan, boasting that he invited a comely wench to Westminster Bridge and there 'in armour complete did I enjoy her upon this noble edifice'. But even Boswell was not always satisfied: his diary reports in 1764, 'Quite agitated. Put on condom; entered. Heart beat; fell. Quite sorry . . .'

Women were less convinced. The French noblewoman Madame de Sévigné warned her daughter that condoms were worse than useless in the bedroom, 'armour against enjoyment, and a spider web against danger'.

Although for some years Mrs Phillips appeared to do a roaring trade, the Green Canister did not make her fortune. She had several marriages and even more affairs, and eventually left England for Jamaica, where she died in 1765.

HOLBORN

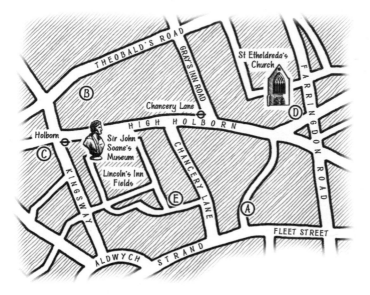

The Flying Pieman

☞ *Fetter Lane*
MAP: *A*

In the early nineteenth century one of the best-known and best-loved characters in the area around Fetter Lane was Peter Stokes, popularly known as 'the Flying Pieman of Holborn Hill'. He covered so much ground so quickly that people used to joke that he flew between locations.

Each day at noon, the pieman would begin his rounds, racing through the streets with his wares and constantly crying out 'Buy! Buy! Buy!' A local diarist, a Mr Harvey, writing in 1863, remembered seeing him as he went about his business:

> **When I was a youngster, the steep roadway from Hatton Garden to Fleet Market was highly attractive to me on account of the 'Flying Pieman', though he did not vend pies, but a kind of baked plum pudding, which he offered smoking hot. In his right hand he held a small circular tray or board, just large enough to receive an appetite-provoking pudding, about three inches thick. This was divided into twelve slices, which he sold at a penny a slice. A broad blunt spatula, brilliantly bright, which he carried in his left hand, enabled him to dispense his sweets without ever touching them. His countenance was open and agreeable, expressive of intellect and moral excellence.**

Peter Stokes was in fact a talented painter. However, he married very young and his income as an artist did not keep pace with the growing needs of a small family, so he supplemented his earnings by spending four hours each day as a street vendor, intent on selling as much as he could.

His paintings may long since be forgotten, but his secondary career as a pieman assured him a lasting place in London folklore.

The First Umbrella in London and How Tea Makes You Flatulent

☞ *Hanway House, 27–31 Red Lion Square*
Map: B

In March 1750, Jonas Hanway became the first Englishman to use an umbrella in London.

He was an intrepid explorer and traveller, and brought back the prototype from Persia, where he had witnessed locals using them to shelter from the sun. *Umbra* is Latin for shade, hence the name 'umbrella'. Hanway realized that these contraptions could be adapted to keep people dry in the rain, so he commissioned the first English umbrellas, which were made of oiled canvas and wood, and became known as 'hanways'.

He tried to encourage use of the umbrella by regularly carrying one himself in the streets of London – a brave move, as he incurred a good deal of ridicule in the process. The city's Hackney-carriage drivers, fearing that they would lose their lucrative wet-weather trade, were particularly hostile. The umbrella, or 'portable roof', was already much used in Paris and cabbies would taunt Hanway with cries of 'Frenchman! Frenchman! Why don't you call a coach?'

Not content with the notoriety caused by the umbrella, he then turned his attention to tea. In 1756 he published *An Essay on Tea*, which became hugely controversial. Hanway was convinced that tea, because of its costliness, was inflicting further hardship on the poor, and that the time taken to make it meant that it was taking its toll on the country's productivity. He also believed it to be detrimental to health, writing, 'this flatulent liquor shortens the lives of great numbers of people'. He claimed too that it caused 'paralitic [*sic*] and nervous disorders', and that it was responsible for making women ugly, and for 'weak digestion, low spirits, lassitudes [and] melancholy'.

Despite his best efforts, tea remained very popular and

developed into something of a national drink. His umbrellas, on the other hand, really took off and have now been keeping the world dry for two and a half centuries.

———— • ————

The Thirteen Club

☞ *Holborn Restaurant, 218 High Holborn*
MAP: C

Among London's most bizarre clubs was the Thirteen Club, founded in the 1890s by journalist and historian William Harnett Blanch. Its aim was to provide an 'antidote to superstition' and at its height it boasted more than 150 members.

It met in Holborn on the 13th of every month. An article written by a guest of Blanch's appeared in the early twentieth century in the *Grey River Argus*, a New Zealand newspaper, recalling a club dinner that took place in the Holborn Restaurant, which sadly no longer exists. The members wore green ties with tiny artificial skeletons in their buttonholes, and a pair of cross-eyed waiters announced that dinner was to start by smashing two mirrors. The diners then

followed an undertaker to Room 13 of the restaurant, passing under several ladders whilst black cats strolled across their paths. In the room were thirteen coffin-shaped tables, each laid for thirteen people. All the knives were crossed and the tables were decorated with peacock feathers, with small lamps lit in plaster skulls and upturned horseshoes. As the diners sat down for their meal they were asked to spill salt before they began eating. Once the meal was finished, they were encouraged to smash the many mirrors in the room.

The club attracted members from all professions, and all the membership fees were distributed to the poor of Southwark.

On being asked to join, Oscar Wilde refused, saying that

'I love superstitions. They are the opponent of common sense.'

'Given the low mortality rate of its membership,' one commentator pointed out, 'it is quite lucky to belong to the club'. However, the Thirteen Club may have been a touch too smug for its own good, as by the turn of the twentieth century it seems to have completely disappeared.

——————— • ———————

The Last Privately Owned Street in London

☞ *Ely Place*
MAP: D

A pair of iron gates separates the quiet little cul-de-sac of Ely Place from noisy Holborn Circus. But very few people know that this street, once the residence of the Bishops of Ely, is not actually part of London. Once you are in it, you are technically in Cambridgeshire and exempt from the jurisdiction of the rest of the capital. Even the Metropolitan Police have no right of entry, unless they are invited in by the Commissioners of Ely Place, the street's own elected governing body, which was formed after a local Act of Parliament in 1842.

Ely Place was bought by the Bishops of Ely as a London residence suitable to their rank after a snub in the thirteenth century when one of their number was refused entrance to their former lodgings at the Temple. They promptly proclaimed their new residence part of Cambridgeshire. The border runs through Ye Olde Mitre Tavern, the local pub, whose licensing hours were, until 1964, controlled by the Cambridgeshire authorities. The pub displays a collection of letters addressed to 'Ye Olde Mitre Tavern, Ely Place, Holborn Circus, Cambridgeshire'.

The Commissioners of Ely Place still employ several beadles, who make sure that the street gates are closed to cars and bicycles after 10 p.m.; they are also responsible for keeping the place clean. Until 1968, the beadles would announce time and weather on an hourly basis from 7 a.m. until 10 p.m., but this practice was stopped after complaints about the noise they were making.

Also in Ely Place is St Etheldreda's Church, the oldest Roman Catholic church in Britain, and one of only two buildings in London that survive from the reign of Edward I.

—————— • ——————

Mousetraps and Hairstyles

☞ *56 Carey Street*
MAP: E

At this address stands a little jeweller's shop called the Silver Mousetrap. It has been in business for over three hundred years and at one time it was *the* shop for rich and fashionable ladies.

In the early eighteenth century women used to spend an inordinate amount of time – sometimes even days – turning their hair into extraordinary sculptures. The style of the day dictated that the hair be piled as high as possible, then plaster birds would be added to make it look as though they were nesting in the hair. The whole creation was stiffened with flour, chalk, dust and pig's fat to keep it all in place.

The problem with such a fantastic creation was that it could easily be ruined after only one day when the lady retired to bed. But some women managed to keep their precious hair-dos in place for weeks by sleeping upright with their hair supported on a mini-scaffolding of pins and pieces of polished wood. This presented its own unique problem, though, as the hair could not be washed or combed, and the sculpted locks would attract mice.

Pest control was still in its infancy in the 1700s, so a visit to the Silver Mousetrap was called for. Here one could buy elegant silver mousetraps to be placed around the head when retiring for the night. By all accounts they were very effective.

BLOOMSBURY
AND FITZROVIA

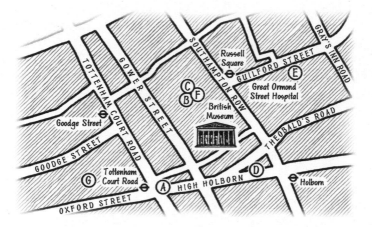

The Great Beer Flood of 1814

☞ *Tottenham Court Road*
MAP: *A*

Londoners have always loved their beer, but it had never seemed
a particularly dangerous passion until, on 17 October 1814, the
Great Beer Flood of London tore through town.

In a bid to capture headlines, breweries at the time often
competed with one another to see who could build the biggest
brewing vat. Some even held opening ceremonies and at one such
event, hosted by the Griffin Brewery, two hundred people were
reported to have dined *inside* the vat.

Standing at the southern end of Tottenham Court Road,
on the corner of Oxford Street, the Meux and Company Horse
Shoe Brewery was one of the most popular breweries in Georgian
London. It possessed a large wooden vat twenty feet high, which
held 3,555 barrels of strong ale. But this gargantuan vessel had
a hidden flaw: eventually the hoops holding it together would
weaken. So it was only a matter of time before one of them failed.
And indeed on that fateful autumn afternoon an 800-pound hoop
fell off the vat and clattered to the floor.

The vat creaked and squeaked, swelled and cracked until finally
it exploded at around 6 p.m. in a delicious outpouring of unfinished
porter. It went smashing through the walls of the brewery, on its
way crashing into several other tanks of beer, which disintegrated
and added their contents to the great swell of ale. The crest of
the wave reached to over fifteen feet as it went gushing into the
surrounding area, the slum of St Giles. Most of the inhabitants
in these poverty-stricken, overcrowded streets were caught
completely by surprise as the torrent flooded through their homes
with such force that two buildings were demolished.

In the midst of all the devastation, the main concern for
hundreds of people was that the beer should not go to waste.
Dozens ran outside carrying pots and pans to scoop it up, while

others just lay down and lapped at the beer cascading past their doors.

When the tide at last receded, the extent of the damage was discovered. Nine people had lost their lives in the beer flood; most of them had drowned, but a few had been knocked from their feet and carried along by the flood, sustaining fatal injuries. It was rumoured that a final victim died the following week of alcohol poisoning, but that story is probably apocryphal.

In a district of such poverty, where any chance to earn money was eagerly grasped, some of the relatives put the corpses of their dead on show in their homes and charged a fee for viewing. In one house so many people pushed inside that the floor capsized, plunging them all into a cellar still deep in beer. Eventually the police put a stop to this macabre side-show, but the funerals of the dead were paid for by the population of St Giles out of the coins left on the coffins by those who had come to see the corpses. The stench of beer apparently lasted for months.

The Meux Brewery Company was taken to court over the accident, but the verdict was that, despite its devastating consequences, the flood had been an 'Act of God' and the deaths, therefore, simply 'casualties'.

————————— • —————————

The Field of the Forty Footsteps

☞ *Torrington Square*
MAP: B

Behind the British Museum stands Torrington Square. It was built in the 1820s on land once known as the Field of the Forty Footsteps, named after a legendary duel that took place here in the 1680s.

According to the tale, two brothers fought each other on this spot over the love of a local girl, who sat watching from a bank at the side of the field. Legend has it that forty of the steps they took during their battle could be seen in the ground for many years afterwards, and the grass never grew back. Both brothers were wounded and they died within days of each other. The girl, racked with guilt, drowned herself in the Thames.

———————— • ————————

Charles Richardson and his Dictionary

☞ *23 Torrington Square*
MAP: C

Charles Richardson was a schoolteacher and a lexicographer. From 1827 to 1835 at this address he wrote his version of the English dictionary, which he called, rather unimaginatively, *A New Dictionary of the English Language*.

In this weighty tome he included some amazing words which seem to have been lost to us over the years:

Addle pate ➤ a foolish, inconsiderate fellow

Beard splitter ➤ a whore master

Buttered bun ➤ lying with a woman who has just lain with another man

Dark cully ➤ a married man who keeps a mistress, whom he visits only at night, for fear of discovery

Dingle ➤ a sex act involving two people in which salmon roe is used as lubrication

Eternity box ➤ a coffin

Fart catcher ➤ a footman who walks behind his master or mistress

Feague ➤ to put ginger up a horse's fundament, to make the horse more lively

Madge ➤ the private parts of a woman

Orgial ➤ a song sung at orgies

Poop-noddy ➤ sexual intercourse

Public ledger ➤ a prostitute [as in open to all parties]

To box the Jesuit ➤ a term for manual pollution [or self-pleasuring]

Tom Turdman ➤ a servant employed to empty chamber pots

The dictionary, it appears, never really caught on.

——————— • ———————

The Ghost Station of the Central Line

☞ *Bloomsbury Court*
MAP: D

The London Underground system includes several now abandoned stations, one of which is British Museum station, which was located at the corner of Bloomsbury Court and High Holborn, and opened in 1900.

There is a long-standing myth that this station was haunted by the ghost of Amen-Ra, an Egyptian princess who died in about 1500 BC. Wearing only a loincloth and Egyptian headdress, she was said to scream so loudly that the sound would carry down the tunnels to the adjoining Holborn tube station. The rumour grew so strong that in 1932 a newspaper offered a reward to anyone who would spend the night there. No one took up the challenge. The story takes a still stranger turn after the closure of the station on 25 September 1933. The comedy thriller *Bulldog Jack*, made in 1935, featured a chase through a secret tunnel that led from the station (called Bloomsbury in the film) to the Egyptian Room at the museum, from where a necklace belonging to Amen-Ra was stolen.

On the very night that the film was released, two women are said to have disappeared from the platform at Holborn – the next station along from British Museum. Strange marks were later found on the walls of the closed station. More sightings of the ghost were reported, along with weird moanings from within the tunnels.

London Underground has always denied the existence of a tunnel from the station to the Egyptian Room, but rumours still abound.

———————— • ————————

A Victorian Pub with 'Snob Screens'

☞ *94 Lamb's Conduit Street*
Map: *E*

The Lamb public house was built in 1729 and named, along with the street, after William Lamb, who in 1577 paid for a new conduit to bring clean water from Holborn. The pub still had one of the original wells in its backyard until the early 1900s.

Today, the Lamb is one of the few remaining pubs in the country with 'snob screens'. These were panels of etched frosted glass installed at head height along the bar in order to prevent well-to-do drinkers from having to watch the common man drinking at the other bar.

The Lamb found fame as a Victorian version of the Groucho Club. Sir Henry Irving, Dan Leno and Little Tich, all stars of Victorian music hall, regularly drank in the place and are commemorated in the photographs that still hang on the walls along with a fine collection of vintage music-hall posters. Charles Dickens, who lived nearby, is also known to have been a customer. In the twentieth century the pub was frequented by the Bloomsbury Group; later the future Poet Laureate Ted Hughes courted Sylvia Plath here. One corner of the pub is occupied by a 'polyphon' – a kind of Victorian jukebox. Apparently it still works, although the playlist is somewhat dated.

———— • ————

The Most Apologetic Building in London

☞ *Thornhaugh Street*

MAP: F

On the wall of the Brunei Gallery of the School of Oriental and African Studies (SOAS) in Bloomsbury is a small plaque unlike any other in London. This particular building has a sign apologizing for being there.

The plaque reads: 'The University of London hereby records its sincere apologies that the plans of this building were settled without due consultation with the Russell family and their trustees and therefore without their approval of its design.'

Much of the land in this area of London was bought three hundred years ago by the Russell family, who later became the Dukes of Bedford. Today it is still managed by the Bedford Estates, although much of it has now been sold off. One of the many bodies to buy land from the family in the 1920s was the University of London, which, as an educational institution, has a right to the compulsory purchase of land. A condition of sale, however, has always been that the Bedford Estates retain the right to approve the design of any new building.

Over the years this proviso has generally been observed, but it appears that in the case of the Brunei Gallery, built in 1988, the design went ahead without having been given the blessing of the estate. So, when the university leased the new building to SOAS, the apologetic plaque was demanded by the Bedford Estates, who specified the exact wording, size and materials to be used.

A quarter of a century later, it remains the only building in London to say sorry.

———— • ————

The Berners Street Hoax

☞ *54 Berners Street*
MAP: G

In 1810 the writer and satirist Theodore Hook bet his friend Samuel Beazley a guinea that he could transform any house in London into the most talked-about address within a week.

Very early in the morning on 10 November, the residents of 54 Berners Street – home of a wealthy lady named Mrs Tottenham – were awoken by the sound of a chimney sweep knocking at the door. He had, the sweep explained, been sent for on a matter of great urgency. A housemaid, annoyed at being awoken, tersely informed him that his services were not required, then she went back to bed.

These were to be the last moments of peace that anyone at 54 Berners Street had for the rest of the day.

Fifteen minutes later a second sweep began knocking at the door, followed by a third and then a fourth. Soon the house was besieged by a dozen such men, all waving brushes and claiming that they had been asked to call at the property as soon as possible.

When the sweeps had eventually been turned away, they were followed by several wagons carrying loads of coal and baskets of fresh fish, which the drivers insisted had been ordered by Mrs Tottenham. By the end of the morning, this trickle of tradesmen had become a tide and included, amongst many others, bakers, coach-builders, shoemakers, doctors, priests and chefs. A dozen pianos were delivered, plus one organ and a coffin. As the day wore on, dignitaries, including the Governor of the Bank of England, the Archbishop of Canterbury, the Mayor of London and the Duke of York, also arrived. So many people were crowded into the narrow street that fights broke out.

Eventually, as the unrest escalated, the police set up a barrier at each end of the street to stop new callers from approaching the house, and finally the crowd began to disperse. But it was late in the evening before the distraught Mrs Tottenham and her servants were left in peace.

Hook had spent several weeks writing an estimated four thousand letters in Mrs Tottenham's name, requesting all manner of people to call at her home. He rented a room in the house opposite so that on the allotted day he and Beazley could watch events unfolding from a safe distance.

Half of London was in uproar over the hoax. Realizing that he had badly miscalculated, Hook vanished and spent the next six months at a friend's house deep in the countryside.

The site of 54 Berners Street is now occupied by the Sanderson Hotel.

CAMDEN AND KING'S CROSS

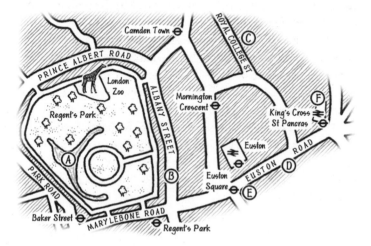

The Five-inch Ruling

☞ *Regent's Park*
MAP: *A*

On a fateful day in January 1867, hundreds of Londoners descended on Regent's Park to take advantage of the frozen lake. At the time ice skating was very fashionable amongst the wealthy, and frozen ponds and lakes were frequently advertised in newspapers.

Despite warnings of thin ice that day, many people made their way on to the lake and began skating. Then the ice cracked and around two hundred skaters plunged into the twelve feet of icy water below. A report in *The Times* described the dreadful scene that followed: 'For many minutes after the breaking of the ice, a multitude of people, amongst whom were several women and children, were struggling in the water, and trying to save themselves by holding on to pieces of ice and most of them screaming in despair.'

Despite the efforts of onlookers and park staff, a combination of heavy Victorian clothing and the general lack of swimming ability swiftly led to tragedy and forty-one people lost their lives.

After the accident, rigid regulations were quickly introduced throughout London's parks. Even though a number of the lakes have now been made very shallow to reduce risk, there is still a ruling which forbids skating in any of the parks unless the ice is at least five inches thick.

The Frank Buckland Diet

☞ 37 *Albany Street*
MAP: B

Here lived the eccentric naturalist, author and surgeon Francis Trevelyan Buckland.

Frank Buckland was a pioneer of zoöphagy: eating animal flesh in the name of science. Anything in the animal kingdom was a potential subject for his research and at his home he would offer such rare delights as mice in batter, squirrel pie, horse's tongue and ostrich.

In 1859, Buckland set up the Acclimatization Society to further the search for new food, which met regularly at the London Tavern. Reports of a dinner party he hosted three years later tell how his guests sampled boiled elephant trunk, rhinoceros pie, porpoise heads and stewed mole.

At his home he kept a menagerie that included a bear, a jaguar, various snakes, parrots and monkeys. He also owned a pet rat that he allowed to run around on the dining-room table.

Buckland also believed that inanimate objects had feelings and began writing a book on the subject. He argued that if a lamp did not burn properly it was sulking and he once punished his luggage by thrashing it.

He died at the age of fifty-four of pneumonia, contracted after swimming in the Thames trying to discover what it would be like to be a fish.

Rimbaud, Verlaine and the Great Fish-slapping Incident

☞ *8 Royal College Street*
MAP: C

In May 1873 the French poets and lovers Arthur Rimbaud and Paul Verlaine rented this house together in what was then called Great College Street.

Rimbaud loved London and wrote parts of his most famous works, *Illuminations* and *A Season in Hell*, here. Verlaine hated London, particularly the food. Oxtail soup appalled him. 'Fie on such a horror,' he wrote. 'A man's sock with a rotten clitoris floating in it.'

The two poets had a tempestuous relationship, not helped by the fact that they spent much of their time drinking. A particular favourite was absinthe; indeed, Rimbaud's sonnet 'Voyelles' ('Vowels') was inspired by his experiments with what he called 'the Green Fairy'.

They fought continually, sometimes with knives rolled in towels. 'As soon as mutilation had been achieved,' according to Rimbaud's biographer Graham Robb, 'they put the knives away and went to the pub.'

Such domestic bliss was never going to last. One day, leaning out of the window, Rimbaud saw Verlaine coming home from the market carrying a fish in one hand and a bottle of oil in the other and started laughing. Verlaine wrote later that when he got upstairs Rimbaud kept sniggering and said he 'looked ridiculous'. Verlaine took exception, slapped Rimbaud round the face with the fish and stormed off, leaving London for Belgium.

A few weeks later, in July, after Rimbaud had pawned his lover's clothes, he set off in pursuit and the pair met again in Brussels. There they had their final row, which ended with Verlaine shooting at Rimbaud, slightly wounding him in the hand and being sent to jail for two years.

Today Great College Street has been renamed Royal College Street and there is a plaque by the front door of number 8: 'The French Poets Paul Verlaine and Arthur Rimbaud lived here, May–July 1873'.

--- · ---

The Abbreviated Handmaidens of St Pancras

☞ *St Pancras New Church, Euston Road*
MAP: D

St Pancras New Church, on the busy Euston Road, was built between 1819 and 1821 in the classic Greek Revival style. It was built entirely of Portland stone and Charles Rossi, a member of the Royal Academy, was responsible for all the statuary.

A week before its consecration, the new church was nearly finished save for a series of beautiful terracotta handmaidens, four supporting each of the north and south porticos. Rossi arranged for the street to be closed off as the statues were delivered on four horse-drawn carts. Eight men were needed to hoist each figure up to its allocated space.

To his horror, Rossi soon discovered that none of the caryatids fitted: they were all twelve inches too tall. With a boisterous crowd enjoying every moment of the attempts to get them into the spaces, Rossi decided upon drastic measures. He arranged for them to be taken back to his studio, where he spent the next two days and nights extracting the twelve excess inches from their midriffs. His explanation for the error was that he could not read the handwriting of his Flemish assistant, who had been responsible for measuring the stone.

On the day of the consecration, the statues were camouflaged with rows and rows of flowers but, despite Rossi's skill as a sculptor, the mistake was too obvious to be completely concealed, so the joins could still be seen. And so they remain today – the abbreviated handmaidens of St Pancras.

———————— • ————————

Tart Cards

☞ *Wellcome Library, 183 Euston Road*
MAP: E

It may at first seem unlikely that one of the world's leading medical history libraries should have any connection with advertising the services of prostitutes, but in fact the Wellcome Library is home to the world's largest collection of 'tart cards'. These are the unique form of advertising used by ladies of the night, and they will be familiar to anyone who has used a central London phone box. For three decades or more, phone boxes have been the usual depository for countless numbers of these small 'business' cards, promising all sorts of forbidden pleasures, from spanking to transsexual encounters, in the privacy of your hotel room or in fully equipped chambers.

The earliest cards in the collection date from the start of the 1980s, and it is interesting to see how these little adverts have evolved over the decades. The first are simple, home-made affairs, photocopies glued on to cardboard, while by the twenty-first century colour-printing and photoshopping had become widely available and the production much sleeker.

Content has changed too, as boundaries have shifted. In the 1980s discretion was still important. The cards contained little more than a phone number and imagery would be restricted to a drawing of a female form. But as taboos fell away, so the cards became more upfront and witty, with revealing photos, images of girls dressed up for roleplay, explicitly jokey straplines and a wider range of services more openly offered. And the ladies too are different. Whereas thirty years ago they were predominantly British, London's 'working girls' today reflect the city's increasingly multicultural character.

In 2003 it was estimated that about thirteen million cards were placed in London phone boxes each year, but their days may now be numbered as new technology continues to reach into every corner of life, and internet and mobile phones provide more modern and efficient ways to do business. Tart cards, however, are acquiring something of a cult status. Tourists are known to take them and send them home as postcards; even kids, bored with trading Pokémon cards, are now collecting them. Once the emblem of a sleazier side of life, they have gradually become part of London folklore.

———— • ————

The King's Cross Airport

☞ *King's Cross Station*
MAP: F

In 1931 one of the strangest airports ever dreamt of very nearly happened. Designed by architect Charles W. Glover, the new Central Airport for London was devised in the form of a giant wheel sitting over the railway sidings just north of St Pancras and would have cost some £5 million.

The idea first came to public attention in an article that appeared in the *Illustrated London News*, which carried an artist's representation showing the eight half-mile concrete runways that formed the spokes of the wheel. The ingenuity of the wheel design meant that planes could take off from and land on the spokes in eight different directions at the same time, and aircraft would taxi around the rim. As 1930s London had no skyscrapers, the approach and take-off would have been free of obstacles.

The airport was to be used for both regular and private flights. Garages built below the runways would be used to store small private planes, which would be brought up by lifts when they were needed. Passengers would also be taken up to the planes via lifts from the terminal buildings at ground level.

So far, so good – but there was a rather obvious flaw in the concept. What would happen if a plane fell off one of the many edges?

The indefatigable Glover, his airport scheme rejected, tried again, this time submitting plans to rebuild the Covent Garden market on the King's Cross site – complete with a helicopter landing pad on top.

ISLINGTON

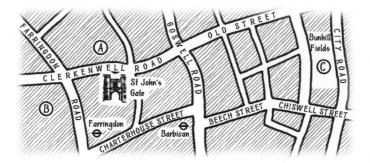

Handel and the Coalman

☞ *Jerusalem Passage*
MAP: *A*

As music became increasingly popular in London after the Restoration, an extraordinary role was filled by Thomas Britton, a coalman by trade.

In the late 1600s he leased a stable on Jerusalem Passage, which he divided into two storeys. Downstairs he stored all his coal, whilst a ladder outside led up to a long, low room where Britton held choral and instrumental concerts every Thursday for nearly forty years. He made no charge, and served coffee at one penny a cup.

The enterprise was so successful that famous musicians such as Handel would gladly perform for this unlikely enthusiast. Handel, who frequently played the harpsichord there, sometimes treated the club with the first performance of a new composition.

Britton was a man of many parts. As well as a lover of music, he was an amateur chemist, dabbled in the occult and was a keen bibliophile. Sadly, he was killed when a practical joke went wrong. One evening in 1714 a member of the audience hired a ventriloquist to tell Britton that he would die unless he fell to his knees and recited the Lord's Prayer. Fall to his knees he did – but it was with a heart attack, and poor Britton died later that night.

The Extraordinary Lady Lewson

☞ *Hatton Place*
MAP: B

'Lady' Lewson, born Jane Vaughan in 1700, was one of eighteenth-century London's more eccentric characters, and many believe she was the inspiration for Charles Dickens's Miss Havisham in *Great Expectations.*

At the age of nineteen she married a rich, elderly merchant, who soon died, leaving her a wealthy widow when she was still only twenty-six years of age.

Her husband's death appears to have caused her to have some kind of breakdown, as for nearly an entire century she barely left their home in Clerkenwell and her increasingly bizarre behaviour became legendary.

Throughout her long life, she continued to wear clothes that were fashionable at the time of her wedding, and she became incredibly superstitious, living in just one room of her rambling house and issuing strict instructions to her servants not to move anything. She would drink tea only out of her favourite cup. Although her life was mostly solitary, she insisted that all the bedrooms be constantly made up in readiness for guests that never came.

She grew obsessed with trying to avoid catching a cold and refused to have any of the windows washed, fearing that the glass would break and let in germs. Over the decades the windows became so grimy and covered in cobwebs that they no longer let in light. She also declined to wash, again fearing that it would cause her to catch cold; instead she smeared her skin with pig's fat and lard, then applied her make-up on top of it.

Nevertheless, somewhat against the odds, Lady Lewson reached the age of a hundred in excellent health and lived on for another sixteen years, dying in 1816, just shy of her 117th birthday.

The Cemetery for Dissidents

☞ *Bunhill Fields Burial Ground, City Road*

MAP: C

This cemetery is the last resting place for a veritable who's who of Nonconformists, as well as some 120,000 fellow dissenters, all of them buried here in unhallowed ground between the late 1600s and mid-1800s.

Among those who lie here are John Bunyan, author of *The Pilgrim's Progress*, Daniel Defoe, who wrote *Robinson Crusoe*, and the poet and artist William Blake, alongside thousands of others who rebelled against political or religious orthodoxy.

So many historically important Protestant Nonconformists chose this spot as their last resting place that the nineteenth-century poet and writer Robert Southey called Bunhill Fields 'the Campo Santo of the dissenters'.

Pilgrims of many types visit regularly to lay wreaths, including Blake Society members, who come every August on the anniversary of the death of the man who wrote *Songs of Innocence and Songs of Experience*, and the poem that became the hymn 'Jerusalem'.

Also buried here is Isaac Watts, the 'father of English hymns'; Susanna Wesley, mother of Charles and John Wesley, whose London home, chapel and grave lie just across the road; the splendidly named Theophilus Lindsey, one of the founders of Unitarianism in the eighteenth century; J. B. Tolkien, grandfather of the *Hobbit* author; George Fox, one of the founders of the Quakers; and the lard-loving 116-year-old Lady Lewson (see page 168).

Buried in 1728 beneath a massive marble chest lies Dame Mary Page. Written on her gravestone is a long inscription recording her excruciating final illness: 'In 67 months she was tapp'd 60 times, had taken away 240 gallons of water, without ever repining at her case or ever fearing the operation.'

When the cemetery was finally declared full and closed in 1853, over a hundred thousand people had been buried in the four-acre site. Evidence of the lack of room can be clearly seen, as every possible space seems to be crammed with headstones.

This sombre spot is now a popular community garden, a haven for stressed workers eager for a brief escape from the frantic pace of City life.

TEMPLE AND BLACKFRIARS

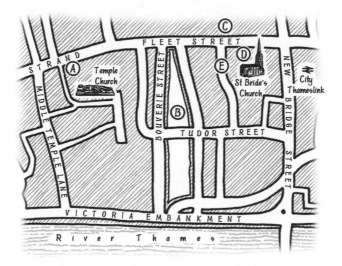

Rackstrow's Museum of Ladies' Bits

☞ *197 Fleet Street*

MAP: *A*

Fascination with the human body burgeoned in the eighteenth century, and the public had a seemingly insatiable appetite for beholding both its inner workings and its possible aberrations – the gorier and more gruesome the better. One of the most infamous places for satisfying this desire was Rackstrow's Museum of Anatomy and Curiosities, which stood on Fleet Street (at the time number 197, almost opposite the entrance to Chancery Lane).

The museum was flourishing by the mid-1700s and contained a wide range of curiosities from the animal kingdom, including the preserved bodies of such exotic creatures as armadillos and the skeleton of a seventy-foot sperm whale; a mummified human body was also on display. But most popular of all was its anatomical collection. Benjamin Rackstrow was a skilled modeller in wax, and he specialized in replicas of the reproductive system, most notoriously female genitals of all shapes and sizes. These particular items were frequently stolen, so two men had to be employed to guard them.

The museum's *Descriptive Catalogue*, published in 1792, lists some of the exhibits visitors queued to see:

> A most curious Figure, singular for Ingenuity, Accuracy and Contrivance; representing a woman about six months gone with Child; in which the CIRCULATION of the BLOOD is imitated by Liquors flowing through GLASS VESSELS, whose figure and situation exactly correspond with those of the natural blood-vessels; also the Motion of the Blood through the vessels of the Navel-String of the Child; likewise the ACTION of the HEART, with the MOTION of the LUNGS, as in breathing.

Two compleat sets of Human Bones placed in uniform order;
the first are remarkable handsome, neat, well-shaped Bones of
a Man, in fine preservation, and very white: the second have
been of a strong muscular Man, and whose Bones were loaded
with an extra quantity of bony matter, rendering them heavy,
uneven, rough, and clumsy.

Rackstrow's was not the only attraction of its kind – Georgian
London had many similar collections, and their existence gives us
an unusual insight into the taste and preoccupations of the age of
Enlightenment.

—————— • ——————

Alsatia, London's Last Sanctuary

☞ *Whitefriars Street*
MAP: *B*

'Alsatia' was a name that came to be given to the precinct of
the former Whitefriars Monastery, lying between Fleet Street
and the Thames, with the Temple at its western end and what
is now Whitefriars Street at its eastern extremity. From the mid-
sixteenth until the late seventeenth century this part of London
was famed and feared for its lawlessness.

In 1538, following the dissolution of the Carmelite order
that gave Whitefriars its name, the jurisdiction of its former land
became unclear. The inhabitants of the area claimed that they
were not subject to the laws of the City of London, and a royal
charter decreed that, because the monks had previously been able
to offer safety to anyone fleeing from justice in the rest of London,
that right of 'sanctuary' still remained in force. So this area was
empowered to grant immunity from arrest and as a result became
the refuge of some of the worst criminals in society. It was called

'Alsatia' after Alsace, the territory constantly disputed by France and Germany.

This was one of the last places of sanctuary in England until the right was abolished by the Escape from Prison Act of 1697. Over time, the area gradually assumed the identity of its neighbours and became a bustling part of the City, although the name 'alsatia' continued to be used to describe run-down neighbourhoods until the advent of the term 'slum' in around 1880.

Alsatia had its own esoteric terms to describe the various criminal professions and characters that lived there. Here are a few:

Abram man or **Tom o'Bedlam** ➤ a thief faking madness

Angler ➤ a thief who used a fishing rod with a hook to lift goods through open windows at night

Dommerar ➤ a man masquerading as a mute

Fencing cully ➤ a receiver of stolen goods

Frater ➤ a rogue who pretended to be collecting for a hospital

Patricio or **Strollers' priest** ➤ a man who performed mock marriage ceremonies

Plater ➤ a prostitute who, when orally pleasuring, would injure her client's testicles and rob him

Polliard or **Clapperdudgeon** ➤ a beggar who preyed on people's sympathy by working with children (not usually his own)

Prigger ➤ a horse thief who went around with a saddle and bridle in case he should spot an untied horse, which he would steal and disguise by dyeing its coat or by adding new marks

Quire bird ➤ a criminal who escaped hanging by turning informer on his fellows

Ruffler ➤ a beggar disguised as a wounded soldier

Strowling mort ➤ an old woman pretending to be a widow

Toppin' cove ➤ the hangman

Upright man ➤ a gang leader

Whip Jack ➤ a beggar claiming to have been a sailor saved from a shipwreck

————— • —————

Spending a Penny

☞ *Fleet Street*
MAP: C

The Public Health Act of 1848, which called for 'Public Necessaries to be provided to improve sanitation', led to one of Victorian Britain's greatest innovations: the public flushing toilet.

The Great Exhibition at the Crystal Palace in 1851 was the first place in England to have 'modern' toilets for visitors. These were installed by George Jennings, a plumber from Brighton, who developed and pioneered the flushing toilet. To offset the cost, visitors were charged one penny for using the toilets, earning Mr Jennings a net profit of £1,790 in only twenty-three weeks and giving rise to the phrase 'to spend a penny'.

Seeing that there was profit to be made, Jennings became increasingly vocal in his campaign for more public toilets, which he called 'halting stations'. Despite his best endeavours, he had great difficulty in convincing the Victorian authorities to adopt them, as the very subject was considered taboo. However, in 1852 the first public toilet in London opened in Fleet Street – opposite the Old Bell Tavern at number 95 – and was an immediate success.

Sadly, nearly all London's original Victorian toilets have long gone, but there are still a few left. Perhaps the best example is the one at St Christopher's Place, Marylebone, in the centre of the square. The aptly named The Attendant, in Foley Street, Oxford Circus, is an example of a restored Victorian lavatory, now a trendy coffee shop. It still has the original urinals, and cisterns to sit on whilst you drink your coffee and read your morning paper.

Nineteenth-century lavatories were luxurious compared to the options for relieving oneself in London in the Middle Ages, when most people simply used a bucket or pot and then threw the contents into the gutter or into the Thames. The idea of public conveniences was not entirely unknown, though. In the twelfth century, if you happened to be walking around in London and were suddenly caught short, you could employ the services of a human lavatory. These were men and women who wore black leather capes and carried a bucket. For the price of a farthing you could sit on the bucket while they stood above and covered you with their cape, thereby protecting your modesty.

The name of only one human lavatory survives: the court rolls reveal that in 1190 a Thomas Butcher of Cheapside was fined for overcharging his clients.

Later, in the thirteenth century, 'houses of office' started to appear and were usually built on bridges. The original London Bridge was equipped with one of these conveniences, while the smaller bridges across the Fleet and the Walbrook also had them, although many consisted simply of wooden planks with holes carved out of them.

More elaborate public privies were also constructed, some with four or more holes, culminating in Richard Whittington's fifteenth-century 'house of easement' or 'long house' over the Thames at the end of Black Friars Lane. It contained two rows of sixty-four seats, one row for men and the other for women, and it had the simplest flushing system of all – the tide. Since the seats were built over the banks of the Thames, the tidal river swept the refuse away out to sea, the journey from riverbank to open water taking between three and eleven weeks. In fact, the word 'sewer' is derived from 'seaward', i.e. taking the excrement to the sea.

Use of these toilets was free, but no toilet paper was provided. Boys patrolled up and down the ranks of seats selling torn-up pamphlets or 'bum fodder'.

Using the city's privies, however, could be dangerous. A quarrel between two men over 'bum fodder' in a privy beside the wall of Ironmonger Lane ended in murder . . .

————— • —————

The Church That Inspired Tiered Wedding Cakes

☞ *St Bride's Church, Fleet Street*
MAP: D

St Bride's is named after St Bridget (Bride) of Kildare, one of Ireland's three patron saints. The present church is the eighth to stand on this site and was rebuilt after the Great Fire by Sir Christopher Wren between 1672 and 1678. It is his tallest church.

Wren added the church's famous layered spire later, in 1701. It originally measured 234 feet but lost its upper eight feet in a thunderstorm in 1764.

St Bride's has long been associated with wedding cakes, and the story goes that in the early 1700s a young man named William Rich, apprenticed to a baker in nearby Ludgate Hill, fell in love with his master's daughter. He proved to have great talent in his chosen trade and when at the end of his apprenticeship he rented a shop opposite St Bride's, it became an instant success. His previous employer, on seeing his former apprentice prosper, finally gave permission for Rich to marry his daughter.

Anxious to impress his new bride and all the guests at their wedding breakfast, Rich looked to the spire of St Bride's for inspiration, creating a multi-layered wedding cake with diminishing tiers. It was a sensation. Word spread and other bakers rushed to follow suit, and before long a tradition that has continued for more than two hundred years was established. St Bride's spire has been known as the 'wedding-cake steeple' ever since.

Wartime bombing in 1940 badly damaged the church, and during renovations the remains of a Roman house were found. There is a museum in the crypt and among the many exhibits is a lockable coffin from the eighteenth century when body-snatching was commonplace (see page 184).

(see page 184)

———————— • ————————

Samuel Pepys and his Paperweight

☞ *Salisbury Court*
MAP: E

The famous diarist Samuel Pepys was born in 1633 in a house in Salisbury Court, just off Fleet Street, and was still living there as a young man when he underwent an unpleasant and dangerous operation.

From early adulthood, Pepys suffered from gout and bladder stones, without doubt because, like many of his contemporaries, he ate too much red meat and drank too much port. With no remedy, and no medicines at this time to offer any real relief, bladder stones were unimaginably painful. Many sufferers acted in desperation, going to great lengths to rid themselves of the agony. In 1625, one man reportedly drove a nail through his penis and then used a blacksmith's hammer to break the stone apart until the pieces were small enough to pass through his urethra.

Surgery in those days was still a potentially life-threatening experience, so Pepys put up with his pain for nearly five years, while he tried every other remedy he could think of. Eventually, he decided on drastic action and on 26 March 1658 the surgeon Thomas Hollyer from St Bartholomew's Hospital arrived at Salisbury Court to remove the stones.

Hollyer first gave his patient a magnificent concoction of liquorice, marshmallow, cinnamon, milk and rosewater, mixed together with fifteen egg whites.

Pepys was next required to strip off his clothes and lie on his back on a table, to which he was then tied down. Hollyer proceeded to insert a metal rod into his penis and up into his bladder in order to 'sound' the stone. Once he had successfully located it, he cut into Pepys's perineum, and finally was able to extract the stone with a pair of pliers. Most of this took place whilst poor old Pepys was fully conscious.

He was then put to bed with strict instructions to stay as still as he could for the next six weeks.

The stone, Pepys wrote later, was the size of 'a goose egg', so he had it mounted on a stone plinth to keep on his desk as a paperweight. The current whereabouts of this magnificent artefact are, sadly, unknown.

ST PAUL'S

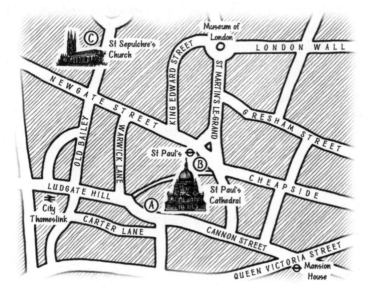

A Foot of St Paul

☞ *St Paul's Cathedral*
MAP: A

During the Middle Ages, the area around St Paul's Cathedral was one of the main markets in London. Traders sold some of their wares by the 'foot of St Paul'. This was an accepted standard measurement of the time and was actually calculated by the length of the foot of St Algar, a statue in one of the columns near the cathedral entrance.

The old St Paul's Cathedral was destroyed in 1666 by the Great Fire of London, so the statue of St Algar was lost. But the measurement survives in our modern foot, equivalent to twelve inches.

——————— · ———————

The Panyer Boy

☞ *St Paul's Underground Station*
MAP: B

In the side of a building on Newgate Street above the steps leading down to St Paul's Underground station, and partly hidden from view, is a stone depicting a naked baker's boy sitting on a pannier, or bread basket. The engraving on the stone states: 'When ye have sought the city round, yet this is the highest ground – August the 27 1688.'

In the Middle Ages this stretch of land was a narrow lane called Panyer Alley, which led from Paternoster Row to Newgate Street and was in the heart of London's bread market. The origin of the carving is uncertain, but it is thought that the stone may commemorate the Panyer Inn, which was destroyed in the Great

Fire of 1666. Whether the Panyer Boy did originally sit at the highest point in the City of London isn't known.

During several rebuildings over the centuries, the boy has been moved many times. For nearly fifty years he sat at ground level, let into a wall between two houses. In 1892, when the wall was pulled down, it was reported that a 'rich American' tried to bribe a workman to steal the stone for him. During the Second World War he was placed in the custody of the Vintners Company for safekeeping, and was installed in his current position in 1964.

The boy – largely unnoticed by today's travellers – has now been sitting on his basket for nearly 350 years.

———— • ————

A Macabre Watch House

☞ *10 Giltspur Street*
MAP: C

Overlooking the graveyard of St Sepulchre's in Giltspur Street, Holborn, this old watch house was built in 1791 in response to the increase in body-snatching that was endemic in the late eighteenth and early nineteenth centuries.

Demand for bodies was high as the only legal way for doctors and students to obtain corpses for dissection was to use the bodies of recently hanged murderers. As demand outstripped supply, the price per body rose to about £50, which was a small fortune in those days.

Body-snatching became so prevalent that it was not uncommon for relatives and friends of the recently deceased to watch over the body until burial, and then to employ a watchman to keep a vigil over the grave to stop it being dug up and robbed. Lockable iron coffins, too, were frequently used, and some graves were protected by a framework of iron bars called mortsafes.

In Edinburgh between 1826 and 1828, the notorious William Burke and William Hare started to commit murder rather than rob graves in order to supply fresh bodies. This method of cutting out the middleman was later copied by the East End-based 'London Burkers', whose similar grisly deeds helped bring about a change in the law. In 1832 the Anatomy Act was passed, which allowed for the legal supply of medical cadavers, finally putting the body-snatchers out of business.

THE CITY AND THE EAST END

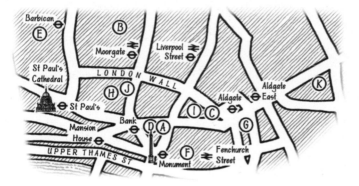

The Devils of Cornhill

☞ *54–55 Cornhill*
Map: A

The church of St Peter upon Cornhill, on the corner of Gracechurch Street and Cornhill, was built by Sir Christopher Wren after the original medieval church was destroyed in the Great Fire of London.

In the nineteenth century plans were drawn up for a new building next door to the church, on Cornhill. The vicar at St Peter's, however, noticed that the proposed development intruded on to the church's land by twelve inches and he immediately protested. The plans had to be redrawn, much to the annoyance of the developers.

In a delicious display of revenge, the architect added gargoyles in the shape of three terracotta devils to the side of the new building that faces the church. If you look upwards you can see them clearly silhouetted against the sky, one of them spitting, one showing its backside and the third sticking its fingers up.

Since their installation, it has always been said that the creatures are taunting the St Peter's parishioners as they supported the vicar's objection. The devil closest to the street apparently bears more than a passing resemblance to the unfortunate clergyman.

When Fanny Became Lillian

☞ *Milton Street*
Map: A

Today its name may be perfectly innocuous, but in the past this small road in the City has sported a much more colourful appellation. It belongs to a large group of London streets whose original names would never receive the blessing of the authorities today – although unintentionally vulgar street names do still crop up, to the amusement of the public and the frustration of local councils.

Arterberry Road in Wimbledon is a constant target for signwriters, who keep painting an 'F' in front. The council is forever replacing the sign, but the local wits simply return to do it again. Meanwhile, in Barnes, the sign for Fanny Road was stolen so many times that in the end they gave it a new name – Lillian Road.

For the schoolboy within, there is Back Passage between Long Lane and Cloth Fair; Penistone Road in Streatham; Cumming Street in Islington; and Clitterhouse Road in Barnet.

While today's connoisseurs of 'rude' streets may have to content themselves with double entendres, in medieval London names were much more explicit about the sometimes vulgar use of the thoroughfare. Some are still with us, such as Addle Street, which means a filthy spot, and Fetter Lane, meaning a place of layabouts or false beggars; but in a more sensitive age others were regarded as simply too rude to continue. Several Pissing Alleys survived the Great Fire of London but fell victim to the *politesse* of the Victorians – one was renamed Little Friday Street in 1848 before being absorbed five years later into Cannon Street. Close by, the shocking Shiteburn Lane – named, of course, for the public lavatories once found there – was transformed into Sherborne Lane.

But first prize must go to this alley just off Cheapside, which was originally called Gropecunt Lane, no doubt reflecting the working girls keen to ply their trade nearby. It was renamed Grub Street in the eighteenth century and then in 1830 became the rather dull-sounding Milton Street.

The Aldgate Pump

☞ *Junction of Aldgate High Street,*
Fenchurch Street and Leadenhall Street
Map: C

The Aldgate Pump we see today was installed in the late 1700s, but this spot has a long history as a watering point. In the sixteenth century the first pump to stand here was erected on the site of the medieval Aldgate well, and over the centuries clear spring water was appreciated here by many for its health-giving mineral salts.

That all changed, though, when in 1875 the inhabitants of the area started to complain about the 'funny' taste of the water and several hundred people died. Investigations revealed this had been caused by calcium leaching from the bones of the dead

in the many new cemeteries in North London through which the stream ran. The following year the problem was solved when the New River Company changed the supply to mains water.

This tragedy seemed to have become a distant memory by the 1920s, when Whittard the tea merchants, seemingly unaware of the pump's history, declared in their advertisements that they 'always get the kettles filled at the Aldgate Pump so that only the purest water [is] used for tea tasting'.

As well as being known for its water, the Aldgate Pump has several other claims to fame. For a long time it was the point from which distances were measured into Essex and Middlesex, and today the road to Southend, the A13, begins here. It is also the symbolic start of the East End, as well as reputedly being the spot where the last wolf in the City of London was killed. The event is commemorated in the pump's brass water spout in the form of a wolf's head.

———— • ————

Cups of Tea, Virgins and Seditious Plotting

☞ *Change Alley*
Map: D

When Londoners were first introduced to tea in the mid-seventeenth century, fabulous and preposterous claims boosted its popularity.

In 1657 Thomas Garway, the proprietor of a coffee house in Change Alley, claimed in a broadsheet advertisement that tea ought to be 'gathered but by Virgins' and that it 'maketh the body clean and lusty'. This miracle elixir also preserves the body 'in perfect health until extreme Old Age . . . vanquishes heavy dreams . . . overcometh the need for superfluous Sleep' and is particularly good 'for Men of a Corpulent Body'.

When the Portuguese Catherine of Braganza married Charles II in 1662 she quickly made tea drinking fashionable amongst the aristocracy and, as a result, the rest of London followed suit. Initially it was sold in coffee houses, and by 1700 there were more than five hundred in London where tea could be drunk. This caused problems for tavern owners, as the popularity of tea meant the public was consuming much less ale and gin; for the same reason it concerned the government, which relied upon taxes on alcohol sales to bring in a constant flow of revenue. Alarmed at such a shortfall, ministers acted quickly to increase the tax on tea.

Despite his queen's fondness for the beverage, King Charles had grown convinced that tea drinking encouraged small groups to meet to talk treason and to plot against him, so on 29 December 1675 he forbade the sale of tea to all private houses. The resulting public uproar, however, forced him to reverse his decision just ten days later, to a collective sigh of relief from the tea drinkers of England.

But by the mid-eighteenth century successive rises in tax had made the price of tea prohibitive for many people and this had the effect of creating a whole new industry – tea smuggling. It also prompted unscrupulous traders to 'cut' tea with other, cheaper ingredients. Some was found to contain ash, molasses and clay, with liquorice being added to impart colour to tea leaves that had already been used. Another trick was to collect used tea leaves and boil them with sheep's dung and ferrous sulphate, then restore their colour with verdigris or carbon black before reselling them.

Luckily, in 1784 the tea-drinking William Pitt the Younger reduced the tax on tea to 12.5 per cent and a year later brought in the Food and Drug Act which included harsh penalties for adulterated tea, thus ensuring the quality of the great British cuppa.

A Wife for 23 Shillings

☞ *Smithfield Market*

MAP: E

For many centuries, Smithfield was London's most important meat and livestock market, but of everything on sale there, surely the most remarkable item was wives.

It is unclear when the custom of selling wives at markets started, but as early as 1553 Thomas Sowdley, a priest of St Nicholas Cole Abbey, in what is now Queen Victoria Street, sold his wife to a butcher. He was one of many married clergymen to face a stark choice between his living and his wife upon the accession of the Roman Catholic Queen Mary I, who restored the law of celibacy for priests after its repeal during the Protestant reign of her brother Edward VI. The good reverend clearly decided his stipend was the more important and sold his wife. Sowdley was then nicknamed 'Parson Chicken' and was pelted with chamber pots and eggs.

More frequent reports of wife-selling began to appear towards the end of the seventeenth century and the practice reached its height during the eighteenth. Typically the sale would be announced in advance, in a local newspaper. It usually took the form of an auction, often at a local market, to which the wife would be led by a halter (usually of rope but sometimes of ribbon) around her neck or arm. Due to the enormous expense of divorce, this was deemed to be an acceptable way of ending an unsatisfactory marriage.

Smithfield's popularity as a venue for such transactions was noted with some alarm in *The Times* on 22 July 1797:

> The increasing value of the fair sex is esteemed by several eminent writers to the certain criterion of increasing civilization . . . and refined improvement as the price of wives

> has risen at that market [Smithfield] from half a guinea to
> three guineas and a half [£300 at today's value].

Wife-selling did not actually become illegal until the early twentieth century. While there is a distinct lack of romance in the idea, there was the occasional 'Barbara Cartland' moment, as the *Gentleman's Magazine* tells us in 1832:

> The Duke of Chandos, while staying at a small country inn
> [while travelling between Newbury and London], saw the
> ostler beating his wife in a most cruel manner; he interfered
> and literally bought her for half a crown. She was a young
> and pretty woman; the Duke had her educated; and on the
> husband's death he married her. On her death-bed, she
> had her whole household assembled, told them her
> history, and drew from it a touching moral of reliance on
> Providence; as from the most wretched situation, she had
> been suddenly raised to one of the greatest prosperity; she
> entreated their forgiveness if at any time she had given
> needless offence, and then dismissed them with gifts; dying
> almost in the very act.

———— • ————

The Smallest Statue in London

☞ *Philpot Lane*
MAP: F

Named after Sir John Philpot, Lord Mayor of London from 1378 to 1379, Philpot Lane is to be found between Eastcheap and Fenchurch Street.

In this little street London's smallest statue can be seen,

situated halfway up the front wall of the coffee shop now occupying number 13. Known as *The Two Mice Eating Cheese*, it was installed in the nineteenth century as a memorial to two builders who were killed while working on the Monument, which stands only a few hundred yards away.

At some time during its construction, the two builders sat down to enjoy their lunch, perched on the scaffolding near the top of the 202-foot (62-metre) column. Apparently one of the men accused the other of stealing his bread and cheese and a fight broke out. They both lost their footing and fell to the ground, dying instantly.

Some time later, after the disappearance of more food, the culprits were discovered – a colony of mice.

——————— • ———————

The Eavesdropping Pub

☞ *The Hoop and Grapes, 47 Aldgate High Street*
MAP: G

The Hoop and Grapes is one of the oldest pubs in London. It is believed that there has been a pub on this site since the twelfth century, and the present building dates from the late 1500s – which is quite an achievement, bearing in mind that the Great Fire of London stopped just fifty yards from its door.

This is one of the very few London pubs still to have a listening tube. It is, quite literally, a tube that runs from the bar area to the cellar and it was installed so that, in more uneasy times, the landlord could continue to listen for treasonable or malicious gossip when he was away from the bar.

There is also a lovely rumour that within the cellar of the Hoop and Grapes there is a blocked entrance to a tunnel that runs from the pub to the River Thames, or even to the Tower of London. If it did exist, it is likely that it would have been used by smugglers.

Dr Butler and his Laxative Beer

☞ *The Old Dr Butler's Head, 2 Masons Avenue*
MAP: H

Here can be found the Old Dr Butler's Head public house, named after Dr William Butler, a shameless fraud and opportunist. He failed his medical exams at Cambridge but nevertheless proclaimed himself a doctor and proceeded to practise some most peculiar forms of healing.

To cure epilepsy he would fire a brace of pistols at his unsuspecting patients in order to scare away the symptoms. As for any poor sufferers of the plague, he would tie a rope around their waist and drop them through a specially designed trapdoor on London Bridge into the icy waters of the Thames below.

Despite his incompetence and the fact that he had absolutely no qualifications, he became Court Physician to James I – a position he achieved by curing the king's constipation with his special medicinal ale. He made this by hanging a thin canvas bag containing senna, polypody of oak, agrimony, maidenhair and scurvy grass in a barrel of strong ale. This proved so successful that he made it widely available, but only to taverns which displayed his head on their signs.

The beer itself had such a violent effect that the resultant arsequake was said to be as loud as the Royal Navy's largest cannon.

The original pub on this site was destroyed in the Great Fire of 1666 but rebuilt soon after. Fortunately, Butler's laxative beer is no longer on the menu.

The Lion Sermon

☞ *St Katherine Cree Church, Aldgate*

MAP: I

St Katherine Cree is the only Jacobean church to have survived the Great Fire of London, and is renowned as the place where Handel used to play the organ. Less well known is a curious event that takes place at the church every year.

The story goes that in 1643 Sir John Gayer, a future Lord Mayor of London, became separated from his travelling companions after been shipwrecked on the coast of Africa. As he wandered alone, he came across a hungry lion, but he prayed for assistance and was left unharmed.

Grateful for his deliverance, Gayer bequeathed £200 upon his death to fund a yearly sermon to mark his good fortune. Sir John died in 1649 and is buried in the church. Since then, 'The Lion Sermon' has been delivered each year to relate his encounter with the lion.

The Soviet Spy Centre
(Moorgate Branch)

☞ *49 Moorgate*
MAP: *J*

Under the guise of the All Russian Co-operative Society (Arcos), the Soviet Union ran a spy ring from this address during the 1920s. It was perceived as an innocuous trade mission and was initially ignored by British authorities. But during the General Strike of 1926, the Soviet government tried to capitalize on the political unrest by donating £250,000 through Arcos to the strike committee. When this was discovered, the British government decided to put an end to Arcos's activities.

With typical Whitehall planning, and in order to look as inconspicuous as possible, on 12 May 1927 fifty uniformed Special Branch officers travelled by tube to Moorgate, where they were met by another hundred uniformed officers who then descended on the building to search it.

Despite the attempts of the Arcos staff to destroy them, more than a quarter of a million documents were seized, as well as crates of rifles. The documents proved to be of no real value, however, and the whole episode resulted in a further strain on Anglo-Soviet relations.

Stalin and the Hostel

☞ *Tower House, Fieldgate Street*
MAP: K

Baron Rowton, aka Montagu William Lowry-Corry, was a nephew of the great Victorian philanthropist the Earl of Shaftesbury. In 1890 he set up a trust to build and run lodging houses for working men.

The first Rowton House opened in Vauxhall in 1892 with 484 beds, offering such facilities as clean sheets, washrooms and ample supplies of hot water. In its first year the beds were let over 140,000 times at sixpence a night. Such success led to the building of five new Rowton Houses, perhaps the best known being Tower House in Fieldgate Street, Whitechapel, which opened in 1902 with more than 800 beds and housed some notable residents.

The American author Jack London described Tower House in *The People of the Abyss* (1903) as 'the Monster Doss House' and recorded that it was 'full of life that was degrading and unwholesome', but other commentators were less scathing. Thirty years later, in *Down and Out in Paris and London*, George Orwell wrote that: 'The best lodging houses are the Rowton Houses where the charge is a shilling, for which you get a cubicle to yourself and the use of excellent bathrooms. The Rowton Houses are splendid buildings and the only objection to them is the strict discipline with rules against cooking and card playing.'

Signing in as Iosif Dzhugashvili, a young Joseph Stalin and his friend Maxim Maximovitch Litvinov (who was later to become Stalin's Commissar of Foreign Affairs) stayed here for a fortnight in 1907, living in true comrade style by sharing a bed at the sixpence charge a night, whilst by day they attended the Fifth Conference of the Russian Social Labour Democratic Party.

Stalin would not have been impressed to know that the building has now been converted into luxury flats.

TOWER HILL

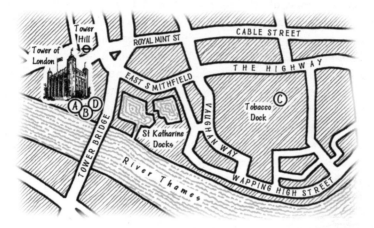

Polar Bears and Smoking Baboons

☞ *Tower of London*
Map: A

The grounds of the Tower of London were once home to the Royal Menagerie. In 1236 King Henry III received three lions from the Holy Roman Emperor Frederick II and, anxious to show them off, housed them at the Tower. Lions remained a fixture here for nearly six hundred years.

In 1252, King Haakon of Norway presented King Henry with a polar bear and there are records of expenses submitted for 'muzzle and an iron chain to hold the bear when out of the water and a long and strong cord to hold it when fishing in the Thames'. A few years later, in 1255, Louis IX of France gave Henry an African elephant, which arrived at the Tower by boat, the first creature of its kind in the country. The contemporary chronicler Matthew Paris travelled to London to see the spectacle. 'The beast is about ten years old, possessing a rough hide rather than fur, has small eyes at the top of its head, and eats and drinks with a trunk,' he wrote. To accommodate the new arrival, the Sheriffs of London were asked to build and pay for a forty-foot-long wooden elephant house, which later found use as one of the Tower's many prison cells.

As the majority of people had never seen such exotic creatures before, for a long time to come there was confusion over how best to care for them. In the early seventeenth century an elephant was presented to James I with instructions to give it only wine to drink in the winter months, to 'keep out the cold'. The poor animal drank over a gallon of red wine a day. Needless to say, it didn't live long, but no lessons were learned: for a further two hundred years the myth prevailed and the elephants were still given their daily carafe.

There was another popular fallacy that ostriches could digest iron, with the result that in 1791 one ostrich died after being fed more than a hundred nails by well-meaning visitors.

Most of the creatures suffered similar fates, as keepers lacked the knowledge to care for them, and the public were unaware of the damage they themselves could cause. It seems that the animals were also encouraged to mimic human behaviour, as an engraving from 1830 shows a baboon puffing on a pipe.

It wasn't just the inhabitants that suffered in the Tower's menagerie. Georgian visitors who passed through its doors were subjected to endless hazards. In the eighteenth century a monkey hurled a nine-pound cannonball at a clergyman and killed him. The wife of the Tower's lion-keeper had her arm amputated when one of the lions, which were allowed to wander around freely, attacked her. It also appears not to have been a particularly pleasant place to work, as Stow's *Survey of London* remarks in 1720: 'The creatures have a rank smell, which hath so affected the air of the place adjoining, that it hath much injured the health of the man that attends them, so stuffed up his head, that it affects his speech.'

One female leopard had a penchant for pickpocketing and thieving, snatching visitors' belongings on a regular basis, as *The Tower Menagerie* by E. T. Bennet, published in 1829, described:

She has always evinced a particular predilection for the destruction of umbrellas, parasols, muffs, hats and other such articles of dress as may happen to come within her reach, seizing them with the greatest quickness and tearing them into pieces almost before the astonished Visitor has become aware of the loss.

Another leopard, who didn't like the intrusion on his personal space, resorted to peeing on people who got too close to his cage. There was also a zebra that was particularly fond of ale and would run off to the soldiers' canteen for a drink. She also allowed children to ride her around the menagerie yard.

In 1799 a School of Monkeys was opened. Visitors were welcomed through its doors until 1810, when a boy's leg was badly bitten.

The Tower menagerie closed in 1835 when the animals were moved to the new London Zoo at Regent's Park.

———— • ————

Executed in an Armchair

☞ *Tower of London*
MAP: B

On 31 January 1941, the German spy Josef Jakobs was captured by the Home Guard when he landed in a field in Huntingdonshire. He was easily apprehended as he had broken his ankle on exiting his plane and was still dressed in his flying suit. He was in possession of £500 in British currency, obviously forged documents, a radio and two German sausages. He was taken to nearby Ramsey police station and later transferred to Wandsworth Prison.

In fact, MI5 had been made aware of the plans for the German's imminent arrival by highly classified intelligence passed to them by the double agent Arthur Owens. Because of the sensitive nature of the information, Jakobs's trial was held behind closed doors in front of a military tribunal at the Duke of York's Headquarters on 4 and 5 August 1941. Jakobs was found guilty of spying and sentenced to death.

His execution took place in the grounds of the Tower of London on 15 August 1941. Due to his broken ankle, he was executed while seated blindfold in a brown leather armchair.

Jakobs's body was buried in an unmarked grave at St Mary's Roman Catholic Cemetery at Kensal Green. All other German spies condemned to death in the UK during the Second World War were executed by hanging at Wandsworth Prison.

Josef Jakobs was the last man to be executed at the Tower of London.

———————— • ————————

The London Noah's Ark

☞ *Tobacco Dock*
MAP: C

In about 1840 a German man named Charles Jamrach came to London and established himself as the world's leading dealer in all kinds of wild animals. His premises in Tobacco Dock became known as 'the London Noah's Ark'. Seamen arriving in the port would deliver an assortment of monkeys, parrots and small animals to his door. Larger creatures, such as elephants, tigers, camels, rhinos and bears, would arrive in huge crates.

Jamrach developed a reputation as a man who could get hold of any creature on earth. Lord Rothschild, who had a private zoo at Tring Park, his home in Hertfordshire, bought a white cougar from him, which he later sent to London Zoo. In 1872, the zoo also paid £600 to

Jamrach, who had agents in the East, for a female rhino from Malacca.

The American showman P. T. Barnum bought animals from Jamrach, who in the early 1880s charged him $360,000 to ship eighteen elephants to New York. One of them was Jumbo, the African elephant who, up to that point, had been London Zoo's most prized exhibit. Initially the zoo refused to sell, but in the end an agreement was reached and Jumbo crossed the Atlantic for an individual price of $10,000.

If you had the cash, you could purchase almost any animal you wanted from Jamrach. At today's prices, a polar bear would cost £900, a zebra £2,000 (incidentally the same price as a camel), whilst a llama would be a snip at £400.

Although most contemporary reports suggest that Jamrach's animals were well cared for, the conditions at his premises would not be acceptable today. Overcrowding was the norm – there are accounts of six thousand parakeets being housed in a single room. Diets were certainly inadequate and often harmful. When animals inevitably died, Jamrach sold their skulls as curiosities.

One particularly notorious incident, however, turned Jamrach into a hero. In October 1857 he received a shipment of animals that included a Bengal tigress. Stressed by a long and difficult sea journey, she broke out of her shipping container and escaped into the streets. A little boy named John Wade approached her and tried to stroke her, but the frightened tigress swiped at him with her paw, stunning him, then grabbed the child and made off with him in her jaws. Jamrach pursued the animal, caught her and put his hand down her throat, forcing her to release the boy.

Despite his bravery, Jamrach was sued by John Wade's parents and had to pay damages of £300.

The event is commemorated by a bronze statue near the entrance to Tobacco Dock, close to the scene of the incident.

The Raven Master and Naughty George

☞ *Tower of London*
MAP: D

The Tower of London is home to England's most famous ravens. Legend has it that as long as the ravens stay at the Tower, Britain is safe from invasion.

It seems that the superstitious King Charles II decided to take no chances, appointing a Raven Master to protect the Tower's ravens and encourage them to stay. The story goes that the first Astronomer Royal, John Flamsteed, was less than thrilled by the monarch's decision, complaining that the birds got in the way of his observations in the White Tower and kept crapping on his telescope.

Today there are eight ravens, which are looked after by the present Raven Master. Their wings are clipped so that they cannot fly away but, despite this, occasionally one does go missing or is sacked.

The Tower ravens are enrolled as soldiers of the Crown and are issued attestation cards in the same way as members of the armed forces and the police. Just like soldiers, the ravens can be dismissed for unsatisfactory conduct. One such was 'Raven George', who lost his appointment to the Crown and was retired to Wales for 'attacking and destroying TV aerials'. And another, named Grog, just disappeared completely, last seen outside an East End pub.

The eight ravens currently residing in the Tower are Baldrick, Bran, Branwen, Gundulf, Gwylum, Hugin, Munin and Thor.

GREENWICH

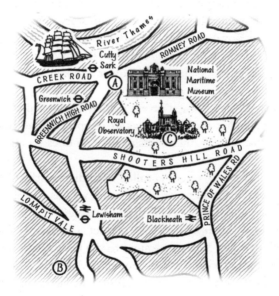

The First Shop in the World

☞ *25 Nelson Road*
MAP: *A*

A shop that stands at the corner of King William Walk and Romney Road – currently occupied by a business called Nauticalia, which sells nautical gifts – bills itself 'the first shop in the world'.

The basis for this bold claim is that the building lies only a few yards from the Greenwich Meridian, at a longitude of 00°00.4'W. It would therefore be the first shop anyone reached if they set off travelling west from the Meridian Line – just a few seconds away.

—————— • ——————

One-legged Cricket

☞ *Algernon Road*
MAP: *B*

In 1848 at the Priory Ground in Lewisham, a team of men with one leg played a team of men with one arm in what was perhaps the most challenging cricket match in history.

Over two thousand people turned up to watch, and the game was immortalized in a report published in an Australian newspaper. 'Novelty was the ruling passion,' it runs, 'nine tenths went merely for the say of the thing.'

This strange fixture was in fact a rematch, as an earlier game had been played between one-armed and one-legged men in 1841; but, the newspaper remarks, 'during this long recess, the great leveller had bowled a large proportion of those who figured on that occasion out.'

All the players were Greenwich Pensioners from the nearby Royal Hospital for Seamen, which from 1692 until

1869 cared for and provided a home for injured sailors of the Royal Navy. They were provided with a 'substantial luncheon' each day, and were equally well catered for after their day's play, with a generous dinner and 'plenty of heavy'.

The betting went in favour of the men with 'two living legs', but in the event it was their one-armed opponents who emerged victorious by a margin of 15 runs. The highest score of the match was 15, and in total twenty-one players were dismissed without scoring at all. Of the one-legged team, five men made ducks (no score).

'The bowling on both sides was generally very wide,' noted the Australian newspaper's critique, 'and the One Legs, in endeavouring to take advantage of it but in the majority of cases missing the object, span round like the final revolutions of an expiring teetotum, and frequently got out.'

With play over, celebrations began and both teams 'marched to the Bull Inn, headed by an excellent band who had been engaged throughout the match. Each man had free passage to and from the Royal Hospital, a glass of grog to drink to Her Majesty's health and ten shillings for his two days' exertions.'

———— • ————

The Time Ball of Greenwich

☞ *Greenwich Observatory*
MAP: C

On top of Flamsteed House, part of the Greenwich Observatory, is an interesting landmark: the bright red Time Ball. This was one of the world's earliest time signals and it was installed here in 1833. It is one of the few time balls anywhere that is still operating today. Its position high above the Thames meant it could be seen from ships in the London docks and out on the estuary, and it was also used as a time check by people on the ground.

Today the Time Ball is automated, but originally it was operated manually by the observatory's astronomers. Each day at 12.55 p.m. the ball rises halfway up its mast. At 12.58 it continues all the way to the top. Then at 1.00 p.m. exactly the ball falls, so providing a completely accurate time signal.

Although noon is the time given by most time signals, 1 p.m. was chosen for the Greenwich Time Ball because the astronomers who calculated the time needed to undertake telescopic observations at noon when the sun was at its height.

At the time when the Time Ball was first in use, only the wealthy could afford to buy watches and clocks. Most people consulted public sundials, with the result that there were different local times across the country, with the eastern side of Britain about thirty minutes ahead of the west. The difficulties created by everyone using their own local time eventually led to the creation of Standard Time based on the Prime Meridian at Greenwich – an event that was hastened by the spread of the railways and the need to create a standard timetable. By 1855 most of Britain had adopted Greenwich Mean Time, although it was 1880 before the transition was complete.

SOURCES AND FURTHER READING

The following books, newspapers, journals, blogs and museums have been invaluable during my research for this book. If you would like to find out more about London, its history, its quirks and its charms, do read on.

Books

Ackroyd, Peter, *London: the Biography*, London: Chatto & Windus, 2000

Barnes, Alison, *William Winstanley: The Man Who Saved Christmas*, Cromer: Poppyland Publishing, 2007

Bettany, George Thomas, 'James Graham', in *Dictionary of National Biography*, Oxford: Oxford University Press, 1992

Boswell, James, *Boswell's London Journal, 1762–1763*, London: Heinemann, 1950

Brocheux, Pierre, *Ho Chi Minh: A Biography*, Cambridge: Cambridge University Press, 2007

Casanova, *History of My Life*, New York: Everyman's Library, 2006

Chancellor, E. Beresford, *Memorials of St James Street*, London: Grant Richards, 1922

Collis, Rose, *Colonel Barker's Monstrous Regiment*, London: Virago, 2001

Garwood, John, *The Million-Peopled City; or, One-half of the people of London made known to the other half*, London: Wertheim and Macintosh, 1853

Gronow, R. H., *The Reminiscences and Recollections of Captain Gronow*, Somerset: R. S. Surtees Society, 1984

Jütte, Robert, *Contraception: a History*, Cambridge: Polity, 2008

Moxon, Edward (ed.), *Essays by Leigh Hunt*, London: 1841

Orwell, George, *Down and Out in Paris and London*, London: Victor Gollancz, 1933

Pepys, Samuel, *Diary*, 30 July 1663; Project Gutenberg, 2009

Robb, Graham, *Rimbaud*, London: Picador, 2001

Starrs, James E. (ed.), *The Literary Cyclist*, New York: Breakaway Books, 1997

Strype, John, *A Survey of the Cities of London and Westminster*, an updated edition of the original *A Survey of London* by John Stow (1598, 2nd edition 1603), London: 1759

Thornbury, Walter, *Old and New London*, Vol. 2, London: Thornbury & Walford, 1878

Topham, Edward, *The Life of the Late John Elwes, Esquire; Member in Three Successive Parliaments for Berkshire*, London: James Ridgeway, 1791

Wheatley, Henry Benjamin, *London Past and Present: Its History, Associations, and Traditions*, London: John Murray, 1891

Whorton, James C., *The Arsenic Century: How Victorian Britain was Poisoned at Home, Work, and Play*, Oxford: Oxford University Press, 2010

Wilde, Oscar, *Epigrams*, Hertfordshire: Wordsworth Editions, 2007

Woodfall, H., *A Journal of Eight Days' Journey from Portsmouth to Kingston upon Thames . . . to which is added an Essay on Tea*, London: H. Woodfall, 1756

Museums, Galleries and Gardens

British Library

British Museum

Chelsea Physic Garden

Handel House Museum

Imperial War Museum

London Transport Museum

Museum of London
Museum of London Docklands
National Gallery
Royal Academy of Arts
Royal Museums Greenwich
Sir John Soane's Museum
Tate Gallery
Tower of London
Wellcome Collection
Westminster Abbey Museum

Newspapers, Magazines and Journals

Bell's Life in Sydney and Sporting Reviewer
Edinburgh Medical and Surgical Journal
Evening Standard
London Magazine
Metro
'The Catastrophe in the Regent's Park', *The Times*, 22 January
    1867
Thomas Garway's Broadsheet Advertisement for Tea, c.1668

Websites and blogs

bowlofchalk.net/1/post/2013/05/London-statues-and-their-
    stories.html
crankedmag.wordpress.com
darkestlondon.com
erinlawless.wordpress.com
ezinearticles.com/9unusualpubnames
faceless39.hubpages.com
forteantimes.com
georgianlondon.com
greatwen.com
historicalromanceuk.blogspot.co.uk

Historic Royal Palaces website
historic-uk.com
inlondonguide.co.uk
mikerendell.com
Museum of Hoaxes
nell-rose.hubpages.com/hub/Strange-and-Bizarre-Tales-of-
    Historic-London
theprintshopwindow.wordpress.com
qna.rediff.com
Shady Old Lady's Guide to London
Sick City Project
stand-and-deliver.org.uk
strangeflowers.wordpress.com
suite101.com
Survey of London online (English Heritage)
the-history-girls.blogspot.com
The Londonist
The Victorianist
thomasroberts.itgo.com
ukattraction.com
writingwomenshistory.blogspot.ie

ACKNOWLEDGEMENTS

My warmest thanks to everyone at Transworld. In particular my editor Henry Vines, whose professionalism, constant encouragement and jolly emails kept the project afloat, and Brenda Updegraff who had the Herculean task of separating wheat from a mountain of chaff. I would also like to thank publicist Sarah Harwood for her infectious enthusiasm, Micaela Alcaino for her wonderful book cover and lovely illustrations, and Patrick Mulrey for his brilliant maps.

ABOUT THE AUTHOR

In a previous life Simon Leyland was a City trader and as such has always been fascinated by the ridiculous and the absurd. Now a full-time writer, he lives in a small cottage on the west coast of Ireland.